R

RANDHURST

Surburban Chicago's Grandest Shopping Center

Gregory T. Peerbolte

The History Press

Published by The History Press
Charleston, SC 29403
www.historypress.net

Unless otherwise noted, images are courtesy of the Mount Prospect Historical Society, Randhurst Archive, donated by the Rouse-Randhurst Company in 1995–96.

First published 2011

ISBN 978.1.60949.147.5

Library of Congress Cataloging-in-Publication Data

Peerbolte, Gregory T.
Randhurst : suburban Chicago's grandest shopping center / Gregory T. Peerbolte.
p. cm.
Includes bibliographical references.
ISBN 978-1-60949-147-5
1. Randhurst Shopping Center (Chicago, Ill.)--History. 2. Chicago (Ill.)--Economic conditions. 3. Chicago (Ill.)--Social life and customs. 4. Chicago (Ill.)--Buildings, structures, etc. 5. Shopping centers--Illinois--Chicago Region--History. 6. City planning--Illinois--Chicago Region--History. 7. Retail trade--Illinois--Chicago Region--History. I. Title.
HF5430.5.C48P44 2011
381'.11097731--dc22
2011007652

I would like to dedicate this book to my family:

Joseph and Darlene Peerbolte and Richard and Edna Legris,
my paternal and maternal grandparents, who lived through some of history's most compelling moments and instilled in me a love for this history at an early age.

Sister Noel Dreska, PhD, OSF,
my great-aunt, who was among the first women in United States history to chair a Physics Department at the university level, for the fear of God (via poor math and science grades), and whose life of intellectualism, spiritualism and creativity was an irreplaceable force.
May Angels Lead You In.

Darwin and Mary Peerbolte,
my parents, whose love, prayers and guidance have protected and sustained me more than anything else throughout the years and make me a little stronger and better every day. And whose visits to all of the out-of-the way museums on family vacations gave me a passion to get involved in museum work.

Matt, Tim and Mark Peerbolte,
my siblings, who also happen to be my three best friends. Thanks for putting up with all those aforementioned museum visits on family vacations.
Go Cubs!

Contents

Foreword

More than forty years have passed, but the memories still follow the same sequence.

Approaching the intersection of Route 83 and Rand Road, the water tower with the distinctive, triangle-enclosed "R" and the large sign with a marquee board come into view. Pulling into the parking lot, we're greeted by colorful signs with stylized pictures of fruit, a handy reminder to help locate the family car when the shopping is complete—Orange Lot, Grape Lot, Apple Lot and such. Walking inside, the first thing we notice are the multicolored, coin-operated lockers that line the corridor walls—orange, yellow and blue—beckoning us to deposit our quarter and unburden ourselves of those heavy coats. Rounding the corner, we get our first glimpse of the "main" portion of the mall. In our case, we usually parked near the entrance adjacent to Carson Pirie Scott, so that first glimpse was of the magnificent blue tile background of Carson's in-mall store entrance, graced by its familiar script logo in antique gold. The mall's lighting level is dramatically low, causing the storefronts to gleam—a wonderful effect. In the center of the mall is the "great dome," afternoon sunlight peering through mod, colored lenses underneath the dome's edge. A mysterious second level (of offices, as it turned out) looms above.

While my parents shop at one of the three anchor stores—Carson's, Wieboldt's and Montgomery Ward, fine department stores in an era of fine stores—the fun really starts for my brother and me. We play on the

Crowds gather outside the blue- and gold-adorned mall entrance to Carson's during the days of the grand opening in 1962.

sculptures that are scattered throughout the mall: cement penguins, walruses and the like. Whether they were meant to be played on is anyone's guess, but played on they were, so much so that they had a patina after just a few short years. Sometimes, of course, the intent of the shopping trip is to buy clothes for us kids, but the prospect of getting to play on the sculptures afterward somehow makes trying on all that corduroy bearable. Then, depending on the time of day, we take a brief moment to relax with a quick meal at the Tartan Tray or the Le Petit Café—or, better still, just grab some candy or popcorn at S.S. Kresge.

This was Randhurst in its early days, as seen through the eyes of a young child—a wonderful, almost magical place. Regardless of age, however, one thing was evident to all: Randhurst had personality.

Many years later, as an adult with an interest in retail history, I learned about Randhurst's very significant historical importance. I learned about Victor Gruen, famed architect and visionary "shopping center sociologist," who designed Randhurst, developed its unique triangular, "pinwheel" design and introduced its most endearing features—the sculptures, space-age benches and quaint European-style pushcarts. I learned about Randhurst's innovative ownership structure, where Carson Pirie Scott, Wieboldt's and

Montgomery Ward (originally under "The Fair" nameplate) joined forces to build the mall, much the way a city's competing railroads would come together to build a Union Station in times past. And I learned about how Randhurst transformed the way a community shopped. No longer was it necessary for northwest suburbanites to travel to downtown Chicago for department store shopping. The stores had come to them!

Time, as is always the case, has a way of changing things, and Randhurst has certainly seen its share of changes. Through the years, however, it has remained a vital part of the community—a place for family and friends to gather together and shop, eat or just enjoy passing the time. And now, Randhurst embarks on a new chapter in its history: a new design, new stores and countless new memories to be made in the future.

With the mall's fiftieth anniversary nearly upon us, it's an ideal time to reflect on the exciting, storied history of Randhurst—pioneering shopping mall, gathering place for two generations and Mount Prospect landmark. This wonderful book will give you an opportunity to do just that. Enjoy!

Dave Aldrich
Pleasant Family Shopping Website

Acknowledgements

I would first like to thank the Mount Prospect Historical Society's board of directors for its support of this project, especially Jean Murphy for her editorial assistance, both for this work and on various publications in my nearly three years at the Mount Prospect Historical Society, and Marilyn Genther and Frank Corry, who, in addition to Jean, have given me professional and personal guidance and a belief that I was capable of handling the execution of this book, which has, at times, been a daunting task.

I am also very much indebted to Cindy Bork, office manager and my "partner in crime" at the Mount Prospect Historical Society, who truly makes my job enjoyable and, perhaps more importantly, has covered for me when I was "in the zone," through all my sudden and unannounced bouts of inspiration for this book. Most importantly, her work ethic has been an inspiration to me and taught me that some of the most important and meaningful professional moments are those that are never seen or acknowledged.

Thanks to Dave Aldrich, whom I consider to be the nation's preeminent retail historian, for his editorial and research assistance and for bringing the fascinating stories of places like Randhurst to the public all over the world. I am honored to have his contributions supporting this work. I would also like to acknowledge other web resources that I have utilized for this book and the work that they do to document retail history, such as deadmalls.com, the online Mall Hall of Fame, Stores Forever, malletin.com, lablescar.com, Nicole Yoguvich's wonderful Lakehurst web resource and many others.

Additional acknowledgements for research go to M. Jeffrey Hardwick, for his wonderful Victor Gruen biography, *Mall Maker*, and his gracious assistance in allowing me to utilize this information.

Additionally, I am grateful to my predecessors at the Mount Prospect Historical Society for realizing the importance that Randhurst has had in the history of our community and for faithfully compiling and documenting the material that made this book possible—and much easier to research.

Thank you to Jere and Katherine Teed for providing me with additional research information.

Also, thank you to Jason Kaplan and Stephanie Pezzella for their dedicated work in the digitalization of voluminous Randhurst materials as Mount Prospect Historical Society Museum interns. It was great working with and getting to know both of you. I hope you enjoy the wonderful careers you surely have ahead of you.

Finally, thank you to the entire community of the Village of Mount Prospect and its dynamic organizations for their support of the Mount Prospect Historical Society. Our community is truly one to be proud of and exemplifies what a community is supposed to be. I thank you for letting me "be a part of it."

My personal acknowledgements go to my extended family of aunts, uncles and cousins. They say you can't choose your family, but if I could, I wouldn't do it any differently. All of you have made life so wonderful for me and, in your different ways, have been an inspiration, and I thank you for encouraging my career.

Thank you to my sister-in-law, Antonia Cruz-Peerbolte; and my "brother-in-law," Adam "Slim" Meier, probably the funniest person I know.

Thank you to my band mates, both past and current, in 5000 South and The Committee Band: Lee Dean, Ryan Leggott, Robert Gates, Donny and Bob Elumbaugh, Garth, Nate and John Johnson, Quincy Spears, Ray Spears, Ed Gallagher, Anthony Williams, Jeff Gall, Brian Winge, Alan Wedgbury, Stacy Mullin, Jordan Digiacomo and so many other wonderful musicians I've performed with over the years. Much like writing a book, performing and writing music requires baring a part of your soul for the world to see. Thanks for your trust and for taking this journey with me. You know a side of me that few would ever understand.

Thank you to Sharon Wahl, my eighth grade history teacher, who let three generations of students at John L. Nash Junior High understand why history is often referred to as a "discipline." Nominating me for the Daughters of the American Revolution history award back in 1998 helped to steer my life more than you may know.

ACKNOWLEDGEMENTS

I am grateful to Norman Townsend, my high school history teacher. I don't know if there is anyone I've met who loves history more than you. Thank you for all of your guidance, and moreover, for teaching me that it is okay to wear your heart on your sleeve when it comes to a passion for history.

Thank you to Martin Kohn, my high school band director. In addition to a love of performing and creating music, you gave me proof that detail, discipline and creativity can work cohesively and will serve you well when applied to all aspects of life. Additionally, you taught me that a sense of humor would be one of my greatest companions and assets as I make the journey. Thank you especially for being one of the first people to believe in my ability as a writer and musician.

Thanks to Jerry Tibstra, my high school art instructor, for helping to cultivate the love for art in my life and letting me know that it is, quite simply, a lot of fun and that life would be pretty dull without it; Carrie Wisehart, my high school English teacher, who, through the written word and the stage, taught me that it is okay to put your emotions into everything you do; and Dr. Jim Paul, professor of history and philosophy at Kankakee Community College. I could never say enough about the impact you had on me intellectually, and I know there are hundreds of your students who feel the same. I remember hearing former students rave about you before taking your courses, and I clearly recall saying to myself, "He can't possibly be that good." There are few times in my life when I have been more wrong.

Thank you to Randy Van Fossan, my professor of ethics at Kankakee Community College, for showing me that just honestly trying to understand something difficult, despite the fear of being wrong, can be enough and has great power in and of itself. In a word: persevere.

Thank you to Jean Cuthbert, professor of English at Kankakee Community College. You were one of the first educators I was challenged by, and it made me a better writer. I never said thank you for that.

Dr. Norman Stevens: thank you for giving me my start in this field and teaching me that no matter how big or small the institution, a passion for intellectual credibility matters.

The Kankakee County Museum Board of Directors and staff—Connie, Jane, Loretta, Robin, Jorie, Sarah F. and Sarah C.—thank you for your patience in seeing me through my stubborn transition from college kid to emerging museum professional. Many times, I wish I knew then what I know now, but I couldn't think of a kinder and more dedicated group of people with whom to begin my career. Keep up the great work in rallying the community around our wonderful museum.

Acknowledgements

Thank you to the Kankakee Public Library and Kankakee Development Corporation and Chamber of Commerce, especially Allison Toth-Beasley, Bill Yohnka and Sarissa Johnson. Please keep up all the great work you are doing to make my beloved Kankakee a great place to live, and thank you for your personal support.

Thanks to Jim Riordan, a good friend and a great author and storyteller. Your work has been an inspiration to me, and I hope to one day follow in your footsteps of success.

I am grateful to William Philpot, history professor at Illinois State University. Through your instruction in environmental and suburban history, you have truly given me a new prism through which to view history that has provided me with immeasurable success in my career. Thank you for the continued guidance you have given me.

JBF, there is something beautiful and breathtaking about the way our lives have intertwined. It may in some way explain my love for history. The passage of time, the places we have been and the things we have seen and felt together, whether spectacular or tragic, whether for moments or for years, will never fail to amaze me. It is amazing precisely because these things *happened.* They happened to no one else but us, in this place and in this time. I adore the fact that we can never live those moments over again, because by knowing, and adoring, the fact that we cannot do so is to have surrendered our love to the ages.

Finally, thank you to all my additional family members, friends, colleagues, professors and teachers throughout the years who are too numerous to list here. Whether we've known each other for days or for decades, you've had an impact on my life that I could not live without.

Introduction

"Unequivocally, Yes..."

So was the response of Karl Van Leuven, Victor Gruen's partner, when questioned by a reporter about a large rendering behind him. Would the massive, space-age structure be the finest shopping center in the United States?

The response occurred in a smoky, frenzied meeting just outside of Chicago in October 1958. The press, local politicians, representatives from three Chicago department stores, architects, attorneys, opposition groups and a "corps of experts" crammed into the modest municipal building of Mount Prospect, Illinois, some twenty miles northwest of the Chicago Loop.

The capacity crowd sat quietly in momentary awe of images of an imposing hexagonal structure with a large domed center, looking like the buildings in the science fiction comics enjoyed by their children. This mammoth building was, in fact, to be a vision of the future. It would stay at a constant temperature year-round, occupy one hundred acres, contain well over one million square feet of space and rise over sixty feet into the air, topped with a majestic dome that would appear to touch the clouds.

The *Mount Prospect Herald* glowingly described the structure in the architectural renderings:

> *"Springtime Forever," a controlled total shopping environment for all-around shopping comfort, is the atmosphere the architects plan for the new Carson, Pirie, Scott and Company regional shopping center in Mt.*

Mount Prospect's Municipal Building, constructed in 1948, was the site of many meetings involving the construction of Randhurst.

The center's original conceptual artwork, seen here, was a bit more "space age" than the final product.

> *Prospect. Three department stores, spaced with groups of smaller shops, would radiate from an enclosed central mall, roofed perhaps with a huge plastic bubble. The entire center would be on two levels to evenly distribute the flow of shoppers and cars. Stores could be entered from either level directly from parking areas. Community facilities would be on the lower level of the central mall, and a restaurant on the upper level. Service activities would be separated by going underground, with basement storage facilities served by a truck tunnel.*[1]

The still unnamed building would become Randhurst Shopping Center. Completed in 1962, the center was hailed as the largest shopping center in the world under one roof and was one of the grandest and most aesthetically striking commercial structures of its day. While shopping centers were popping up throughout the major cities of the United States, Randhurst was an experiment and perhaps one of the greatest actualizations of what these structures could, and would, be in terms of their commercial power, their architectural power, their aesthetic power and their cultural power.

Randhurst combined a number of elements of suburban shopping centers that would make it a first in the long line of malls and shopping centers that had a lasting and undeniable impact on American culture. From its inception, Randhurst had stories to tell. As Randhurst itself was developed, and later evolved, so too did attitudes about shopping, commercial structures and why we shop where we shop. Randhurst both led and followed these trends during its half century of existence. It was and is a reflection of the times.

With the backing of the booming Village of Mount Prospect, the quiet ground of farmland in Mount Prospect would soon begin to stir, as it had so many times during the 1950s. While the story of Randhurst began during this period, the story of its location and origins began a century earlier.

1

"We Will Have State Street in Mount Prospect"

For almost the first century of its existence, the community of Mount Prospect was identified as a rural burg in proximity to the city of Chicago. The area was originally settled by various native tribes, most notably the Pottawattamie. The first settlers came to the area in the 1840s. These were largely "Yankees," who traversed westward through what was then known as America's Great Northwest. Many of these original settlers stayed only briefly and continued moving west.[2]

The community received its permanent settlers in the form of German Lutherans, who were immigrating to the United States in droves from areas in what was then Prussia, such as Hanover and Schleswig-Holstein. Interestingly, these immigrants came to the United States for many of the same reasons as the Puritans had some two hundred years earlier. In their drive toward unification, the Prussian states were becoming increasingly militarized and secularized. Some traditional Lutherans felt that the church was modernizing too rapidly and sought refuge where they could practice their faith freely in its traditional form. The community of Mount Prospect marks the establishment of St. John's Lutheran Church in 1848 as a benchmark date.

In addition to the arrival of permanent residents, transportation was essential to the growth and vitality of the village. Its proximity to Chicago via the Chicago and Northwestern Railway served as an advantage. The challenge faced by early developers of the area was establishing a railway depot that was acknowledged by the railway company. This would ensure Mount Prospect's survival. Despite the fact that the village was not officially incorporated until nearly 1917, the construction of a train station essentially allowed the community to exist for nearly half a century prior to this.

The first major development of the area occurred in the early 1870s and closely followed the laying of the railroad. Mount Prospect was platted and promoted by Ezra Eggleston. Eggleston was also responsible for naming Mount Prospect, in typical late nineteenth-century booster fashion. Because the area sat on some of the highest land in Cook County, and because Eggleston wanted to convey the idea that there would be great "prospects" for the future, this optimistic name was coined. His salesmanship was not an isolated incident. Many nearby communities, both new and existing, adopted names that were evocative of relaxed, rural landscapes. In the latter half of the nineteenth century, major American cities were industrializing at a rapid rate. In the name of progress, sanitary concerns were often overlooked or ignored completely. Chicago was, unfortunately, famous for this concept due to contemporary accounts of the meatpacking industry, such as, whether real or imagined, in Upton Sinclair's novel *The Jungle*. As a result, cities were viewed as not only physically unclean but also morally deplorable. Developers such as Eggleston hoped to capitalize on this notion by cultivating outlying communities that conveyed unspoiled, pastoral imagery.

Eggleston was also responsible for building a railroad depot in the village. As previously stated, this was an essential addition to the community. The train station was a flag stop, meaning that trains would only stop at the depot if flagged down by the stationmaster. This also, admittedly, occurred due to the fact that Eggleston had not consulted the railway company before constructing the depot.

Even though the Great Chicago Fire of 1871 made the idea of living outside the crowded and combustible city popular, the devastating Panic of 1873 made selling land outside the city a fool's errand. So while Eggleston's venture was unsuccessful, his legacy is still alive and well in the Village of Mount Prospect today, and history would prove him correct in his prediction that land on the rail lines outside of the city would one day become desirable and profitable.

In the years approaching the turn of the century, the founding German families took over Eggleston's defunct venture. While the early villagers had a large degree of control over who settled in the community, there was a desire among them to make Mount Prospect an attractive place to live. Among these early residents were John C. Moehling, who owned a general store and managed the village post office; John Meyn, who was recruited as the village "smithy"; William Wille, who operated a cheese factory and was later responsible for the construction of many of the early public and private buildings in the community; and William Busse, a Cook County commissioner who operated multiple businesses, including an automobile dealership and hardware store, and used his political savvy to serve as Mount Prospect's biggest booster.

The first major move to "open up" Mount Prospect to non-Germans was the formation of the Mount Prospect Improvement Association in 1911. The association existed as a quasi-governmental organization, since the village lacked the three hundred citizens necessary to be considered for incorporation. The Improvement Association, funded by private donations, was responsible for a number of upgrades to the village. An early map of Mount Prospect boasted that it was an "ideal location for suburban homes, on a high point 100 feet above Chicago" with "good drainage in all directions." Life in the suburban town would be made easier by "eighteen trains daily, 42 minutes from city" with "better service under consideration." The developers also took pains to let potential buyers know

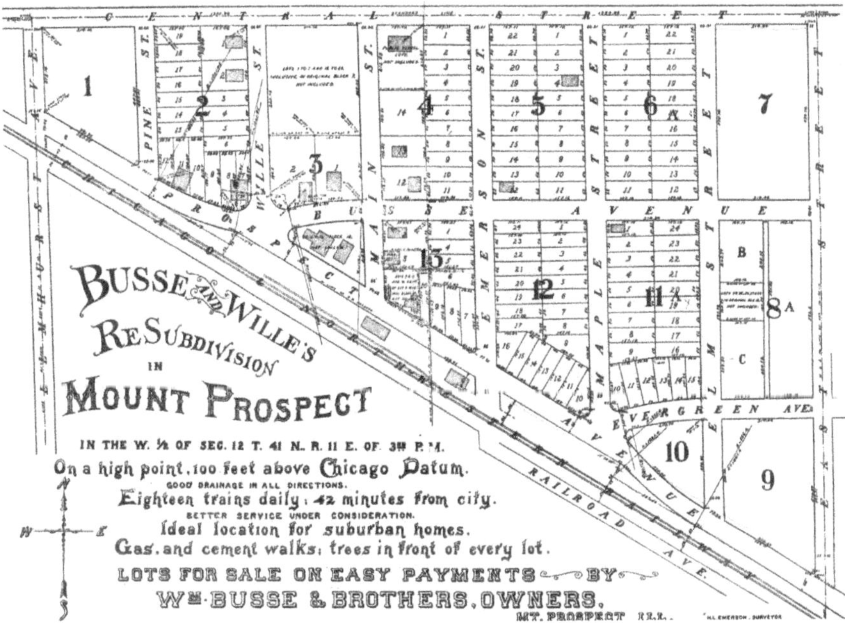

"Busse and Wille's ReSubdivision" advertised the village's proximity to Chicago, "gas, and cement walks; trees in front of every lot" and "Eighteen Trains Daily."

that the progressive community also contained "gas, and cement walks; trees in front of every lot."[3]

Among the first major improvements was to pave and grade the streets of Mount Prospect. For many years, these streets were little more than dirt trails. The association hired Frederick Biermann, a teamster from nearby Elk Grove Township, to come to Mount Prospect to construct and maintain the new streets, as well as to install gas streetlights. It may surprise some to learn that a teamster, who was able to control a team of horses, possessed a highly specialized skill. With the advent of the automobile, the early villagers knew that a system of well-maintained streets would be vital to the growth of the community. The story of Commissioner William Busse's Buick dealership also implies that embracing the automobile would be commercially healthy for Mount Prospect. According to one account, Busse first saw the automobile on a trip to Chicago. He immediately realized the potential of these machines and entered the store to inquire about establishing a dealership of his own. He was told that that particular Buick dealership had exclusive licensing over the whole of Cook County, and a dejected Busse left. Sometime later, as Busse worked on the roof of one of his buildings, a man climbed up the ladder and identified himself as a Buick representative who had heard of Busse's interest in establishing a dealership and would now allow him to do so. As the story goes, Busse signed the papers while still on the roof, and one of the first automobile dealerships in the northwest suburbs was born. Busse Buick would be a driving force behind life in early Mount Prospect.

Another addition to Mount Prospect under the early founders—and later, the Improvement Association—was the implementation of public services and institutions. The earliest of these was the construction of a public school. William Busse was again a leading force in this movement. While today it would seem impossible that any forward-thinking community would object to the creation of a school, it once proved to be a hard-fought battle. Throughout the nineteenth century, the notion of public education was a controversial subject. In a nation that had formed its identity, in part, because of the resentment of taxes, the idea that residents of a community could be taxed to pay for the education of other children was a hot-button issue of political debate. In the 1840s, an upstart Illinois politician named Abraham Lincoln argued passionately for the creation of a public school system in his political campaigns, citing his own lack of access to a public school.

Half a century later, Mount Prospect experienced a similar battle. After much debate, Busse secured the support of the community to construct a school. Busse then decided, along with William Wille, the general contractor hired to construct the school, to expand the building beyond its original size and add separate cloakrooms for the students. Wille, also a supporter of a good school for the fledgling community, agreed to make these improvements at his own expense. Despite this, the residents, who were originally opposed to the school, were infuriated upon hearing the news of these extravagant additions and immediately rescinded their support for the project, even going as far as threatening a lawsuit. William Busse, being a Cook County politician, clearly knew the fine art of political maneuvering. He put an end to the opposition by "accidentally" running into an opposition leader on the way to a meeting and making his case for the expansion of the school building and why the establishment of this building would be beneficial to the community's growth.

The building that caused such a stir among the early residents still exists today, preserved by the Mount Prospect Historical Society as a permanent addition to its museum campus. It appeared that Busse's foresight was correct, as the school building did have a ripple effect on the creation of other community entities. Among the varied organizations that called the Central School home, and which continue to thrive today, are the Mount Prospect Fire Department, St. Paul's Lutheran Church, the Mount Prospect Public Library, the Mount Prospect's Women's Club and one local Boy Scout troop. The Central School, rather appropriately, was also the site of the signing of the village charter in 1917, when Mount Prospect was officially incorporated.

While they likely did not know it at the time, these founding families were paving the way to make Mount Prospect an ideal suburban destination. They knew quick and easy transportation to the city through avenues such as the Northwest Highway and the Chicago & Northwestern Railroad were essential to the success and growth of the village. They also realized early on that automobiles would not long remain "rich men's toys" and sought to provide motorcars, service and a reliable system of paved roads. They further knew that public institutions such as schools were a hallmark of any community that wanted to attract residents and that these schools should not hesitate to provide the best possible education. At the same time, frugality was an important value to these residents. They realized that while public institutions were necessary and important, extravagant spending and taxation would be the quickest way to dissuade new residents.

Mount Prospect, however, was certainly not unique in its march toward the future. Countless communities throughout the country were taking these vital, while perhaps unintended or unconscious, steps toward suburbanization.

The majority of outlying towns such as Mount Prospect were taking organic steps toward becoming what we know as suburbs. However, some towns in the area were being meticulously planned with a suburban vision. The community of Riverside, located directly west of the city, was designed by renowned landscape architect Frederick Law Olmsted, who was the mind behind Central Park and the Biltmore Gardens. Riverside was designed by Olmsted with painstaking deliberation. The community was characterized by curved, winding parkways and liberal use of trees and plants (which were planted meticulously in order to appear random), with a central train station (the railroad being virtually the only straight line in the town) that included a central business district and, perhaps most importantly to Olmsted, a large public green. The idea of a majestic "promenade" in the suburban neighborhood was paramount to its creation. Olmsted not only felt that it was a great asset to any community but also that ignoring its creation was to ignore central tenets of Western civilization and democracy. In the papers from the planning of Riverside, he wrote of its lofty implications:

> *The promenade is a social custom of great importance in all the large towns of Europe. It is an open-air gathering for the purpose of easy, unceremonious greetings, for the enjoyment of change of scene, of cheerful and exhilarating sights and sounds, and of various good cheer, to which the people of a town, of all classes, harmoniously resort on equal terms as to a common property. There is probably no custom which so manifestly displays the advantages of a Christian, civilized and democratic community, in a contra-distinction from an aggregation of families, clans, sects or castes. There is none more favorable to a healthy civic pride, civic virtue or civic prosperity. As yet, the promenade has hardly begun to be recognised as an institution in Chicago, but there is no doubt that it soon must be, and it is evident from the present habits and manners of the people, that when once established, the custom will nowhere else be more popular or beneficent in its influence.*[4]

Olmsted certainly practiced what he preached in regards to the use of public space. He vehemently defended the promenade. In his mind, a true public space could not coexist with a private one. When he discovered plans to construct a private residence on the green, Olmsted lashed out at the president of the Riverside Company in a letter, telling him unabashedly, "I can not express to you how much I am shocked and pained to hear that such a suggestion could for a moment be entertained. It is not a matter for argument. It sets aside all at once the study which we have given to your enterprise as of no value and breaks the plan in its most vital point." The massive shopping center to be in Mount Prospect years later would carry much influence from Olmsted's work.

The thousands of communities around the country that are now considered suburbs took different paths toward this end. While the majority of towns, such as Mount Prospect, knew that they were somewhat reliant on a metropolitan area, they never considered themselves a direct extension of it. These towns considered themselves independent communities and, moreover, sought to remain as such. Thus, their suburbanization took place slowly and encountered a number of battles and controversies along the way. Other towns, such as Riverside, became classic suburbs from their inception and depended on daily commuters to Chicago to flock to outlying areas to raise their families. Furthermore, Riverside was characterized by the establishment of a public "promenade," as well as a central and, more importantly, contained business district. While communities such as Mount Prospect and Riverside evolved somewhat differently, their fates would in many ways be intertwined. Whether created intentionally, suburbs were on their way, and by the dawn of 1960, Mount Prospect was among the leading suburban communities in Chicagoland. Ripe and ready for growth, Mount Prospect village manager Harold Appleby told the *Chicago Tribune* that this growth would not be taken lightly. If Mount Prospect was going to build a shopping center, it was not to be a small affair: "Our residents moved here because they want to live in a high class residential community. And that's the way we want to keep it."

"We will have State Street in Mount Prospect," he vowed.[5]

2

"This Is the First Time This Has Happened Anywhere in the Country"

Conceptualizing Randhurst

In early May 1958, a large helicopter flew lazily over the Chicago metropolitan area. On board was John T. Pirie Jr., head of one of Chicago's oldest and most prominent department stores, Carson, Pirie, Scott & Co. Pirie was accompanied by company officers and members of the board of directors. The copter flew north to Waukegan, west to O'Hare Field, south to Joliet and east to Hammond, Indiana. Following the flight, Pirie remarked that the purpose of this excursion was to visually survey the vastly growing outlying areas of Chicago and what he described as the city's "inevitable expansion." He stated:

> *We wanted to see firsthand what is happening and the significance of the toll roads and expressways now under construction…We viewed many interesting sites and were particularly impressed with the excellent road network provided by Route 83 and Rand, Foundry and Euclid Roads, immediately northeast of Mt. Prospect. We believe this network offers the best available opportunity for an advantageous pattern of traffic to a regional shopping center of the size we contemplate.*[6]

At that time, the area Pirie spoke of was the site of one the oldest existing farms in Mount Prospect, the Burmeister Farm, originally cultivated as the Miller-Tegtmeier and Runde Farms. The farm was still active at the time of

This aerial view of Mount Prospect, circa 1956, is what Carson's officials saw from their helicopter. Note the areas of open land that are quickly being replaced by subdivisions of homes filled with families and consumers.

the aerial survey and had been continuously farmed since the latter years of the Civil War. The eighty-acre tract, surrounded by heavily traveled roadways and as yet free of any commercial or residential development, certainly would be ideal for Randhurst, the building that would soon become the world's largest shopping center under one roof.

Carson, Pirie, Scott & Co. originated in Amboy, Illinois, in 1854 as a business founded by Scotch-Irish immigrants Samuel Carson and John T. Pirie. By the end of the Civil War, the business had moved to Lake Street in Chicago. In 1890, Robert Scott joined as a partner, and the firm changed its name to the familiar moniker. By the turn of the century, the company had two downtown stores at State and Washington and Franklin and Adams Streets, each employing approximately one thousand people. In 1904, the company moved into its beloved Louis Sullivan–designed building at State and Madison. Throughout the twentieth century, its retail operations continued to grow, and by the time of its proposed construction of Randhurst, it operated eleven stores in Chicagoland and employed eight thousand people, reporting an estimated $150 million in annual sales.[7]

By August 1958, Carson, Pirie, Scott & Co. had successfully purchased the Burmeister Farm and entered into negotiations with the Village of Mount Prospect to have the land annexed to the community. Annexation was vital for the completion of Randhurst. With the land becoming a part of the village, it would have access to the services it would require to construct and maintain the massive center, including water, electricity and police and fire protection.

Mount Prospect was one of a number of communities in the northwest suburbs that retailers such as Carson, Pirie, Scott & Co. saw as an untapped resource in terms of sales potential. Mount Prospect and its neighboring communities had changed from small, rural towns into bustling suburbs almost overnight.

Shortly after its purchase of the Burmeister Farm, Carson's appointed one of its "top men" to supervise the planning, development and construction of the proposed center. The *Mount Prospect Herald* reported in September 1958 that "the plans of Carson, Pirie, Scott & Co. to develop a large shopping center north of Mt. Prospect took one step nearer realization this week" when divisional vice-president Harold R. Spurway was named to a position in which he would supervise planning and real estate development. Spurway told the newspaper:

> *The balance of this year will be devoted to producing an organization to complete the project. During that time, we hope to complete our engineering and economic studies. During 1959, actual production of the building sketches will be completed and our real estate and leasing program will be finalized. Perhaps by the fall of 1959, the first spade of earth will be turned. However, the start could be delayed until early in 1960. After we get started, it will take 16 to 18 months to complete the center. Carlson boasted that the new center would be "largest by double" of any center operated by Carson's, including nearby Edens Plaza. Carlson also expressed his desire for the center and company "to be a part of Mt. Prospect."*[8]

While Carson's proposed shopping center would by no means be the first in Chicago, the company was determined to make it Chicago's grandest. By 1958, Carson's already had a number of stores in the Chicago suburbs. As testament to the population density of the suburbs, the aforementioned Carson's-operated Edens Plaza was less than twenty miles from the proposed location in Mount Prospect.

While the helicopter hovered over the area, on the ground, Mount Prospect flourished. Many residents traveled down Rand Road to nearby

An early architectural rendering of Randhurst, circa 1960.

Des Plaines for a quick bite to eat at a popular drive-in restaurant called McDonald's, and a Mount Prospect resident employed at nearby Weber-Stephen Metal Works spent his free time crafting the perfect outdoor grill.

Mount Prospect, along with its neighbors in the northwest suburbs, was growing at an immense rate in the 1950s. While the community had experienced increases in population prior to this period, the size and scope of the growth was unprecedented. In sheer numbers alone, the population increased from 4,009 in 1950 to 18,906 in 1960, representing expansion by over 470 percent in a decade—this from a village that took over half a century to reach the required 300 residents necessary for incorporation.

School construction also skyrocketed during this period. Like Busse and Wille before them, the community leaders of the 1950s knew that quality schools would attract families to the community. After the construction of the one-room Central School in 1896, Mount Prospect did not build another school until 1927. In the 1950s, six schools were constructed in the village. In addition to schools, other community organizations were established in this decade. Residents enjoyed a public library, which was expanded in 1950, and a new park district, established in 1955.

The network of roads alluded to by Pirie also played a large role in Mount Prospect's development and was another factor in attracting Randhurst to

Lincoln Junior High, seen here circa 1955, was one of six schools constructed in Mount Prospect from 1950 to 1960. Its students would come to play an active role in aspects of Randhurst's promotion.

the village. The early founders, again, knew that embracing the automobile and supporting it with a system of good roads would be beneficial for growth. Mount Prospect and the surrounding communities were supported by the construction of the Edens in 1951 and the Northwest Tollway in 1960. Not only did this allow rapid access to Mount Prospect, but also, and more importantly, it allowed working commuters, many of whom owned more than one automobile, and their families to settle, live and ultimately shop in the village.

Many of these new suburban residents were returning GIs from the Second Great War and, later, the Korean Conflict. Government assistance allowed these veterans to attain a college education and inexpensive housing. America's victory in the war allowed for a booming economy that provided well-paying, plentiful jobs. These jobs also gave the young families a larger expendable income. Thus, the demand for goods skyrocketed, as did the demand for housing, schools and services.

These facts were certainly not lost on the developers of the Randhurst. In a brochure that was distributed to potential Randhurst tenants, they are laid out rather frankly:

> *Mount Prospect was selected as the location for Randhurst Center after detailed study of surveys and reports on accessibility, economic stability and buying power of the surrounding communities. The results showed an active buying market...a trade area not affected by any other regional shopping center...an existing road system which is more than adequate. The 100 acre Randhurst site is located at a heavily traveled intersection...This is approximately 22 miles from Chicago's Loop. The two newest high speed expressways in Northern Illinois are both within minutes of Randhurst.*

The prospectus also describes the chief role played by the automobile in the commercial success of Randhurst:

> *The automobile has come to play such an important role in modern living—especially among the big two-car family population in the Randhurst Trade Area. The ideal highway network surrounding and leading to Randhurst makes it necessary to consider the population within reach of the center on the basis of driving time.*

By the time of Randhurst's proposal, the Mount Prospect Village government had already dealt with some of the growing pains associated with the development of shopping centers, especially in matters involving the zoning of these structures. In a 1955 meeting of the zoning board discussing the proposed rezoning of an area that "appeared to be developing into a shopping center," the board declared that "the parcels within our control could assist in such development." The zoning board, ahead of a unanimous vote approving the development, concluded, "Judiciously located shopping centers, rather than sprawled out commercial areas, are desirable in a well-organized Village Plan."[9]

The village government had good reason to be supportive of shopping centers and also to want to control their location. The most important justification for shopping centers was the contribution of the sales tax to the village coffers. The aforementioned demand for affordable housing and ample services was accompanied by an expectation of low property taxes. The sales tax proved to be a great compromise; high property taxes were the quickest way to scare potential residents into a nearby community where the taxes were lower. Thus, these taxes were extremely competitive, given the proximity of Mount Prospect to its neighboring northwest suburban communities. The sales tax, being accompanied by a good or service, was much easier for residents to swallow. Moreover, the sales tax was not exclusive to Mount Prospect residents. Anyone who wished to shop in Mount Prospect would be contributing to the village. This was perhaps Randhurst's greatest appeal to the village. Both the village government and Randhurst developers were counting on the fact that a massive shopping center would draw citizens of other communities. What's more, these shoppers were expected to come, not from Chicago, but from the growing suburbs farther to the northwest. As seen in the diagram of the trade area in the Randhurst prospectus, Randhurst's targeted buying power was farther away from the city. The prospectus, somewhat arrogantly, notes this fact:

> *The projected trade area does not extend to the closer-in suburbs and northwestern corner of Chicago. It may be easily assumed that this area holds a considerable potential. However, it is not included in the figures being presented. It is a plus factor for you.*

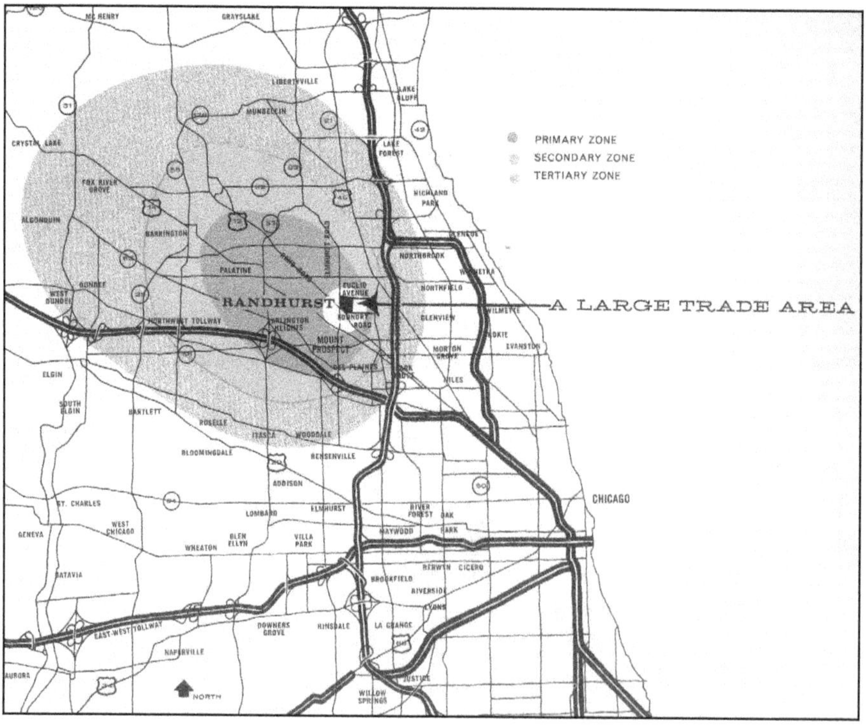

Today, one shopping center expecting to draw from these huge boundaries would be laughable. Note that the trade area is "aimed" away from Chicago.

Homeowners, however, while completely willing to drive to a shopping center and, as such, contribute to the sales tax revenue, did not want to live in the high-traffic, and at times dangerous, areas surrounding shopping centers. Thus, the call for "judiciously located" shopping centers was also a contributing factor in establishing a large, concentrated shopping complex.

By 1959, these many factors were cemented into the development of Randhurst, so much so that the project was ambitiously expanded. A February 26, 1959 *Chicago Tribune* article made the startling announcement that the project would include the partnerships of two Chicago retailing powerhouses that were also Carson's biggest competitors. Wieboldt's Department Stores and Montgomery Ward & Co.'s "The Fair" store entered into negotiations with Carson, Pirie, Scott & Co. to form a joint corporation. Like Carson's, these companies also had storied histories tied to Chicago retailing and made their homes on State Street.

While Montgomery Ward and The Fair had recently merged, both department stores had a rich history in Chicago dating back nearly a century. The Fair, according to retail historian Dave Aldrich, was originally described by the *Chicago Tribune* as a "little jewelry shop with a 16 foot frontage on State St.," established in 1880. The article gave E.J. Lehmann, the store's founder, the distinguished, though effectively unprovable, title of "originator of the modern department store." Interestingly, it was also noted that Lehmann was credited with being the first to price merchandise to the odd penny, now a standard practice of retailing. In 1890, the company had gained national prominence when the *New York Times* reported that The Fair was entering into a "big commercial scheme" to construct the largest department store in the world, which would encompass half of an entire city block and rise twelve stories above State, Dearborn and Adams Streets. By 1925, the company had gone public, and the controlling shares were purchased by Sebastian S. Kresge, owner of the store that bore his name. In a twist of fate, S.S. Kresge would later operate a large store at Randhurst, despite no longer owning The Fair. S.S. Kresge's would, years later, become K-Mart. Kresge administered the store with a "hands-off" approach, allowing existing management to operate the stores. Eventually, ownership of The Fair was transferred to the Kresge Foundation, which later sold it to Montgomery Ward. In the years leading up to the Great Depression, The Fair followed its competitors and began establishing stores in outlying suburbs. All was quiet with the company until the 1950s, when shopping center construction began in full force, with The Fair establishing stores in the new Chicagoland shopping centers of Evergreen Plaza and

This picture of the exterior of The Fair store at Randhurst, circa 1962, was included in a promotional photo package produced by Victor Gruen Associates.

Old Orchard. Montgomery Ward took control of The Fair shortly after the opening of Old Orchard in 1956. In a bold move, the company announced shortly after its entrance into the Randhurst Corporation that The Fair would represent the company at Randhurst.[10]

Montgomery Ward was even older than The Fair. The *Encyclopedia of Chicago* recounts:

> [It] *was established by Aaron Montgomery Ward in 1872. Ward, a New Jersey native, arrived in Chicago in 1866 to work for Field, Palmer & Leiter, the large dry-goods business that would, interestingly, become Marshall Field & Co. After selling Field's products in hard-to-reach rural areas for several years, Ward decided to create an easier means to market merchandise. In 1892, Ward and brother-in-law George R. Thorne invested $2,400 in a new mail-order business. Boosted by orders from members of the Patrons of Husbandry (or "Grange"), the Midwestern farmers' association for which it served as an official supply house, the business grew rapidly. In 1874, the catalog was 32 pages long; by 1876, a 152-page Ward catalog listed 3,000 items. The slogan adopted in 1875, "satisfaction guaranteed or your money back," proved to be appealing to consumers, who used Ward's catalogs to order all sorts of goods, including clothing, barbed wire, saddles, windmills, and even steam engines. By 1897, annual sales had reached $7 million and the catalog was nearly 1,000 pages long. In 1900, there were about 1,400 workers at the company's Michigan Avenue headquarters; 10 years later, when annual sales stood at nearly $19 million, Ward employed more than 7,000 Chicago-area residents at its huge new facility along the North Branch of the Chicago*

River. As branches were added around the country, annual sales grew to over $100 million by 1920. The company entered a new era in 1926, when it decided to follow the lead of Sears, Roebuck & Co., its main rival, by opening retail stores. By 1931, there were more than 530 Montgomery Ward stores across the country. Led by Sewell Avery, the company continued to grow during the Great Depression.[11]

Avery, a staunch capitalist, was famously evicted from his office in 1944. During the war, Montgomery Ward supplied the Allies with everything from tractors to auto parts to workmen's clothing—items deemed as important to the war effort as bullets and ships. However, Montgomery Ward chairman Sewell Avery refused to comply with the terms of three different collective bargaining agreements the United Retail, Wholesale and Department Store Union hammered out between 1943 and 1944. In April 1944, after Sewell refused a second order from the National War Labor Board, Roosevelt called out the Army National Guard to seize the company's main plant in Chicago. Sewell himself had to be carried out of his office, quite literally, by National Guard troops. By December of that year, Roosevelt was fed up with Sewell's obstinacy and disrespect for the government's authority. Reportedly, Sewell's favorite insult was to call someone a "New Dealer"—a direct reference to Roosevelt's Depression-era policies. On December 27, Roosevelt ordered the secretary of war to seize Montgomery Ward's plants and facilities in New York, Michigan, California, Illinois, Colorado and Oregon. In his announcement that day, Roosevelt emphasized that the government would "not tolerate any interference with war production in this critical hour." He issued a stern warning to labor unions and industry management alike: "Strikes in wartime cannot be condoned, whether they are strikes by workers against their employers or strikes by employers against their Government." Sewell took the fight to federal court but lost.[12] After the war, Montgomery Ward continued to operate as a retail powerhouse.

Wieboldt's, a Chicago-area chain of department stores, was founded in 1883 by William A. Wieboldt. By the beginning of the 1910s, the Wieboldt's store on Milwaukee Avenue in Chicago employed about seven hundred people and grossed $3 million in annual sales. The company added new locations over the next few years. By 1930, Wieboldt had five stores with a combined $21 million in sales. The company enjoyed another growth spurt after World War II, and by 1960, there were ten Wieboldt's stores grossing a combined total of over $80 million in annual sales.[13] It was reported

This photo of the Wieboldt's store at Randhurst, circa 1962, was also part of the promotional photo package produced by Victor Gruen Associates.

that Wieboldt's stores were known for "their good values, unpretentious merchandise, and multilingual sales staff. The stores were especially popular among ethnic, working-class shoppers who could not afford or did not like to shop at the big downtown department stores." Wieboldt's slogan was: "Where You Buy With Confidence!"[14]

These companies represented three of Chicago's strongest merchandisers, and together they would form the region's largest and strongest shopping center. About this time, the corporation announced it would name itself, and the center, Randhurst, after Rand and Elmhurst Roads, two of the largest arteries to the center. By this time, Carson's had purchased, and the village had rezoned, an adjacent 28-acre parcel of land, bringing the grand total of the site to 108 acres. Three competing enterprises entering into such an agreement was unprecedented and shocked many Chicago commercial real estate observers.

The analogy of "warring" department stores was not lost on the *Chicago Daily News* when it announced that "Carson's, Wieboldt's, The Fair Foot the Bill for Close Combat" and told its readers that

> *triple barreled department store competition will be highly concentrated here...with the opening of Randhurst Shopping Center. Banging away at each other from the corners of the triangular center on Rand and Elmhurst Rds. will be three old rivals...Though competitors, the stores are equal partners in financing the $21,000,000 center...Isn't it unusual for three department stores to develop a shopping center together? This is the first time this has happened anywhere in the country, says George O'Neill, the center's manager. Don't the three retailers, then, have misgivings about the venture? No, declares O'Neill.*[15]

As General Manager O'Neill stated confidently, "It all boils down to whether you think there are enough customers in the area."[16]

The *Mount Prospect Herald* also noted that

> *such an agreement is believed to be unique in commercial development of this sort, and assures that emphasis will be along mercantile lines rather than as a real estate project. A spokesman for the stores said that each of the three is actively working on specific details. These details and the name of the center will be announced shortly. Lack of precedent for many features of the arrangement makes progress somewhat slower than usual, but the opening date is tentatively planned for late 1961.*[17]

Assurances that the agreement of the three retailers would not become a "real estate project" were due to a fear of a new phenomenon that was occurring in many suburban boomtowns: sprawl. A common practice of shopping center developers was to purchase large tracts of land for the construction of centers. Upon completion of the center, there was typically an abundance of unused land, which would be sold off to subdevelopers to construct apartments, out-parcel stores, gas stations and other businesses that could effectively "feed" off the presence of a sizable center. This would also provide a quick return to developers who usually had to wait for some time for a shopping center to start realizing substantial profits. Brightly lit, unsightly "strip mall" developments especially drew the ire of nearby residents and municipal governments.

The *Tribune* reported that the agreement would call for the establishment of a new corporation in which the three companies would share ownership of the land and buildings equally. Each would lease space for its own needs from the corporation, which in turn would manage and operate the center. It was again reiterated that the "arrangement is believed to be unique in shopping center developments and assures that emphasis will be on mercantile rather than real estate lines." The preliminary plans, which called for 800,000 square feet of floor space to be divided among the three main stores and projected perhaps forty additional stores, still fell short of what Randhurst would eventually become.

The article also noted that by this time, Carson, Pirie, Scott & Co. already operated five branch stores, four of which were in shopping centers; Wieboldt's operated seven stores, one of which was in the nearby Harlem-Irving shopping center; and Montgomery Ward, as a result of its recent expansion in acquiring The Fair, operated twenty-three stores around the country, with twenty located in shopping centers.

Randhurst was not without its opposition. Interestingly, the strongest came from another developer. Literally weeks before Carson's approached the Village of Mount Prospect, developer Dan Serafine had laid out plans for a regional shopping center to be built at the intersections of Rand and Central Roads, less than a mile from the proposed site of Randhurst. Serafine's attorney argued in front of the village zoning board that the high number of traffic accidents should deter the village from constructing Randhurst, to which the board chairman replied, "Merchants would not be interested in the location unless there was a lot of traffic." The Mount Prospect Chamber of Commerce had originally opposed the project but had rescinded its objection by 1962, shortly before the center opened. Mount Prospect residents had, and continued to, rely on local merchants for their day-to-day needs, but they were leaving Mount Prospect to make significant purchases elsewhere. A Mount Prospect resident, when questioned about the initial impact of Randhurst, stated, "When Randhurst opened up it had a big impact. I mean, it was bringing people in from all over. You talk about shopping—this is where we did our shopping, really, at Randhurst. Before that, we shopped in Arlington Heights or Des Plaines. We really didn't shop that much in Mount Prospect." Another longtime Mount Prospect resident stated that her family would travel as far away as Six Corners in Chicago, where Irving Park Road and Cicero and Milwaukee Avenues intersect, to shop before the construction of Randhurst. Shoppers at Six Corners were overseen by an imposing Art Deco Sears, Roebuck & Co. store, which remains to the present day.[18]

As the months passed, the plans for what would become Randhurst Center grew more and more ambitious. These ambitious plans required an ambitious mind to realize them. The contract to build Randhurst was awarded to the office of a commercial architect and city planner named

Victor Gruen. By 1962, Gruen was among the most celebrated architects of the day; he was even a household name by some newspaper accounts. A profile of him in the *New Yorker* once stated, "One of the best known architects in the country is a middle-aged, barrel-chested man named Victor Gruen. Distinguished by heavy brows, unruly dark hair, and a no less unruly Viennese accent, Mr. Gruen is sort of an intra-continental guided missile, maintaining offices in five cities."[19]

"An intra-continental guided missile." A dignified portrait of architect Victor Gruen, circa 1965. *Image provided by Victor Gruen Collection, American Heritage Center, University of Wyoming. Used with permission.*

It could be easily said that Randhurst and Gruen had been waiting for each other. As early as 1948, in what would be an almost verbatim description of Randhurst, though the center was a decade and a half from being realized, Gruen proclaimed:

> *It is our belief that there is much need for actual shopping centers—market places that are also centers of community and cultural activity. We are convinced that the real shopping center will be the most profitable type of chain store location yet developed, for the simple reason that it will include features to induce people to drive considerable distances to enjoy its advantages.*

Gruen had not always been so celebrated. Like the recipe for so many classic American success stories, Gruen's story mixed sadness, adversity, hard work, a bit of luck, impeccable timing and unflinching optimism. So who was Victor Gruen?

3

"Mr. Gruen Is Sort of an Intra-Continental Guided Missile"

The Architect

Herbert M. Kraus & Co.
For: Victor Gruen Associates, May 12, 1960
Contact: Mort Kaplan
For Immediate Release

Because of its increasing volume of activities in the Midwest, Victor Gruen Associates, internationally known firm of architects, engineers, and planners, has opened offices at 222 N. Michigan Avenue, Chicago. The firm, which employs 250 persons, also maintains offices in New York and Los Angeles.

Raymond O. Brinker will head the new Midwestern office, which will occupy one-half the fifth floor at the Michigan Avenue address. The Chicago staff will number about twenty-five persons.

Victor Gruen Associates, widely renowned for such landmarks as Northland and Eastland shopping centers, Detroit, and Southdale, Minneapolis, has many current projects in the Midwest. The firm is architect for the $20,000,000 Randhurst regional shopping center in Mt. Prospect, Ill., of which Carson, Pirie, Scott & Co., Montgomery Ward & Co., and Wieboldt's are joint sponsors.

Currently Victor Gruen Associates is working on a number of large projects in the Midwest such as downtown redevelopment for the cities of

Green Bay, Wisconsin and St. Paul, Minnesota; department stores in St. Paul, Minnesota (Dayton Co.) in Appleton and Sheboygan (Prange); in Cleveland (the Parmatown branch of the May Co.) and shopping centers in Minneapolis (Brookdale Center) and E. Peoria, Ill. (Highland Hills); and an office building for the Colorado Bank in Denver.

Victor Gruen Associates developed a plan five years ago for downtown Fort Worth, Texas, which attracted world-wide attention. The proposal called for strict separation of private auto, bus, truck, and pedestrian traffic. The planning activities of 100 cities have been influenced by this plan.

More recently the firm proposed a master plan for Kalamazoo, Mich. When Kalamazoo in 1959 tore up one of its main streets and became the first city in the country to build a permanent downtown mall, merchants, planners, city offices and writers from all over the nation focussed [sic] *on the city.*

In Chicago, Victor Gruen Associates designed the Merchants and Manufacturers Club, a restaurant in the Merchandise Mart with a seating capacity of 1,100.

Partners in Victor Gruen Associates are Victor Gruen, R.L. Baumfeld, Karl O. Van Leuven, Jr., Ben H. Southland, and Herman Guttman. All activities of the firm are guided by these men.

Mr. Gruen is active as an author and speaker. He is co-author of Shopping Towns, USA, just published by Reinhold, which has been widely heralded as the most authoritative and complete work on the subject of shopping centers. His articles have appeared in numerous popular and professional journals including Life, *The* New York Times Magazine, Progressive Architecture, Harvard Business Review, *and many others.*

In his definitive biography of Victor Gruen, *Mall Maker*, historian M. Jeffrey Hardwick stated, "The Randhurst Shopping Center represented the height of Gruen's retailing dreams in suburbia. With over one million square feet of stores and three department stores meeting under a giant dome, Randhurst was an object lesson in the economic dominance of the suburbs."[20] By the time of Randhurst's construction, Victor Gruen was perhaps the nation's foremost commercial architect, which was quite an impressive accomplishment given the story of Gruen's unlikely emergence in the American commercial market.

Gruen's rise to fame was a classic American success story juxtaposed with two of the nation's most trying experiences. Gruen was born Viktor David Gruenbaum in Vienna, Austria, in 1903 to what he described as a typical, liberal Viennese family. His father, Adolf, was an attorney who had many clients involved with the vibrant musical and cabaret theater scene. While his family was Jewish, Gruen was not particularly involved in the faith. One of his architectural partners once explained, "Victor was much more of a Viennese than a Jew," while Gruen himself, completely omitting any identification as a Jew, later ranked his varying identities, quite colorfully, as "adorer of the female, Socialist, humanist, environmentalist, architect, businessman, philosopher."

Vienna at the time of Gruen's birth was also largely viewed as the birthplace of modernism, with Europe's leading artists, architects, musicians and writers calling Vienna home in the latter years of the Austro-Hungarian Empire. Though by the time Gruen had come of age the creativity had turned into political turmoil as Europe became involved in the Great War, he still felt he was living in the "center of intellectual and cultural life in Europe." He graduated from the prestigious Realgymnasium in 1917 and pursued an architectural degree at the Vienna Academy of Fine Arts. Sadly, Victor's father, Adolf, died suddenly in 1918, and as the family's only son, young Victor left school to provide for his mother and sister. Despite the fact that the recent collapse of the Austro-Hungarian Empire left Vienna in a state of what was described as "chaotic social and economic conditions," Gruen fortunately found work in the architectural firm of his godfather, Melcher and Steiner. While he found little satisfaction in his work initially, he spent his twenties and thirties devoted to the theater and Socialist politics, two of his greatest passions, which had been an intricate part of his young life. Gruen's love for the interplay between actors and audience

Gruen, self-described "adorer of the female, Socialist, humanist, environmentalist, architect, businessman, philosopher," certainly had an entertaining self-image. *Image provided by Victor Gruen Collection, American Heritage Center, University of Wyoming. Used with permission.*

and his fervent belief in Socialism would have major implications for his future projects—shopping centers most especially.[21]

By the 1930s, Gruen was beginning to come into his own as an architect, establishing his own architectural firm in the apartment he shared with his wife, Lizzie, whom he met through his involvement with the theater. Several of his new clients included leading Viennese department stores. A London review of one of his designs termed it "one of the most modern and interesting designs," citing Gruen's creative use of innovative materials, lighting and mirrors.[22] As Gruen himself would later advise retailers, "A good storefront is one of your best salesmen."[23]

At the same time, Gruen's politically charged satirical performances in the coffeehouses and cabarets of Vienna were openly critical of Hitler and his expansionist aims. It was reported that Gruen and his comrades often satirically dressed in Nazi uniforms and mocked Hitler's speeches, attacking the tenets of National Socialism and German expansionism.[24] Gruen was no doubt horrified when, on March 12, 1938, Nazi Germany officially annexed Austria. As the Nazis marched into Vienna, Gruen was caught unprepared, and like many in the Jewish community, he refused to believe that his beloved Vienna could turn on him. The Viennese Fascists, sympathetic to the Nazis, confiscated Gruen's car, seized his architectural firm and had him jailed. After he was able to secure his release, Gruen hid in the home of Lizzie's mother, while the couple desperately searched for a sponsor through Ruth Yorke, a theater acquaintance residing in New York City. In the meantime, Gruen destroyed evidence of his involvement with opposition groups. At last, an American, Harry Lowry, agreed to sponsor the Gruens, and they fled Vienna on June 9. A theater friend disguised as a Nazi storm trooper saw to it that the couple arrived at Vienna's airport without incident. As the plane ascended toward Zurich, Switzerland—the first leg of the couple's long journey—Gruen quietly thanked God for letting him escape with his life. Many Viennese Jews would not share Gruen's fate: an estimated 65,000 out of an estimated 175,000 who lived in the city in 1938 were systematically slaughtered in the Holocaust.[25] The same week that the Gruens narrowly escaped Vienna, another refugee and Viennese intellectual by the name of Sigmund Freud also fled his native Austria. Freud wrote, in sentiments quite likely shared by Gruen, "The triumphant feeling of liberation is mingled too strongly with mourning, for one had still very much loved the prison from which one had been released."[26]

Gruen, in a moment that would come to define his trademark optimism, saw great promise in the bustling New York City upon his arrival, despite the conditions under which he came. He was a thirty-five-year-old refugee, unemployed and bankrupt, carrying no possessions (save his Viennese T-square and a few of his plays), and he spoke no English. As if this weren't enough, America was racked in the midst of the Great Depression. Gruen, however, looked to the future brightly, recalling, "I have nothing with me, no problems, everything is ahead, the world is open." It was said that despite the towering Empire State Building, Rockefeller Center and Chrysler Building and the massive public works projects such as Triborough Bridge and Westside Highway, Gruen was most impressed by Broadway's Great White Way and Frederick Law Olmsted's masterpiece, Central Park. As Gruen biographer M. Jeffery Hardwick described this transitive moment:

> *Built for nearly opposite reasons, Broadway's brashness and the park's peacefulness shared one important aspect: They were loved and used by the public. On a larger scale than Vienna's parks and theaters, Broadway and Central Park welcomed all New Yorkers. The two places—one built with public funds and the other erected by private capital—provided entertainment for all comers. In his later retail projects, Gruen would try to unite these two seemingly contradictory experiences.*[27]

Gruen was, again, fortunate to find work in the city not long after his arrival. In 1939, as the world stood on the brink of war, the 1939 World's Fair opened in Queens. Despite the punishing Great Depression and foreboding clouds of war, the fair was an exhibition in optimism. Television, air conditioning, fluorescent lighting, Lucite, nylon, diesel engines, color film and the "miracle mineral" asbestos all made their debut at this fair. Gruen worked on the production team that produced General Motors' "Futurama," the fair's most popular attraction. The exhibit gave riders a glimpse of a miniaturized, ordered city of the future in 1960, with the automobile as the fitting star of the show. Gruen later credited the exposition's popularity as setting the scene for the national highway program of the 1950s.

Gruen also found time to successfully pursue his theater interests during this period, establishing the Refugee Artist Group, which presented several Viennese cabaret–style offerings on Broadway. The group was supported by leading American artists, such as composers Richard Rodgers and Irving Berlin, singer Al Jolson and novelist Edna Ferber. A passionate letter of support for the group was written by a fellow refugee, declaring, "This new type of theater concerns itself with political and psychological problems that should be presented to the American public in its battle against the forces of fascism and race hatred. Yours very truly, A. Einstein."[28]

Shortly after the fair, Gruen caught another break when he was strolling down Fifth Avenue and, by sheer coincidence, ran into a Viennese acquaintance, Ludwig Lederer, whose family ran several high-end leather goods stores in Paris, Berlin and Vienna before the outbreak of World War II in Europe. Lederer now sought to design a store on glamorous Fifth Avenue and hired Gruen on the spot.[29] Throughout the war, Gruen continued to design storefronts to much acclaim and later moved on to designing freestanding department stores on the outskirts of bustling cities and towns. By the end of the war, Gruen had moved on to designing something of a new-fangled concept: the shopping center. While the concept had existed in America and Chicago since the 1910s, and in philosophical ways harkened back thousands of years to the Greek *agora* and medieval marketplaces, it enjoyed a new prominence in the automobile-driven, postwar American economy.

Gruen's earliest descriptions of his ideal shopping center in many ways mirrored what was actualized in Randhurst. Shortly after Gruen relocated to Los Angeles, he produced a proposal for his ideal vision of a shopping center. The proposal, which appeared in *Chain Store Age* in 1948, well over a decade before the completion of Randhurst, laid out Gruen's ideal center. The center of his fifteen-building complex would contain a seven-story warehouse that would serve as a central "monumental landmark." The center would include massive parking areas forcing the visitor to experience the center itself as a pedestrian to "relieve the intense nervous strain under which we all live" and provide "psychological comfort" to the shopper. In addition to scores of retailers, an intricate facet of the proposal included "rest benches, flower beds, drinking fountains, tree groups…and announcement boards." In a sentence, the entire shopping center would have "the character of a large park surrounded by shopping facilities."[30] Gruen also thought that the shopping center should be a center of civic and cultural activities. In addition to stores, Gruen proposed the construction of a band shell, exhibit hall, nursery, civic hall, wading pool and first aid station, as well as dining rooms, lunch counters and a number of kiosks, which were inspired by traditional vendors, who sold goods directly from their carts in open-air markets in Gruen's native Vienna. His aim was quite clear. The inclusion of these aesthetic amenities would encourage shoppers to "prolong their stay at the center."[31] Moreover, Gruen sought to make shopping the hub of cultural life in suburbia, which was criticized for its rapid and unbridled growth and little attention to cultural institutions. In Gruen's own words, the addition of these amenities would "impress the center's facilities deeply into the minds of the people living in

The Fair Court at Randhurst, 1962, fit Gruen's qualifications of having "the character of a large park surrounded by shopping facilities."

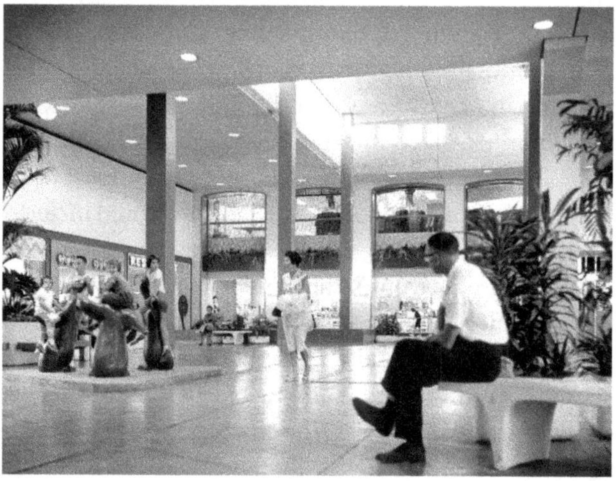

Wieboldt's Court at Randhurst, 1962, exhibits Gruen's demand for "cultural enrichment and relaxation" in his shopping centers.

a wide surrounding area." Overall, Victor Gruen's ideal suburban shopping center would offer the height in "cultural enrichment and relaxation."[32]

Gruen's Randhurst and his notion of shopping centers blended the best aspects of capitalism and socialism. Much like Olmsted's village green in Riverside and his masterpiece, Central Park, the notion of a public space around private enterprise proved successful beyond Gruen's wildest dreams. In fact, as Gruen would later claim, it may have worked too well. Much like Olmsted and his precious village green, Gruen would later be forced to defend his public spaces in the face of private development.

By 1950, Gruen had established his own architectural firm and was enjoying increasing fame in postwar America. Several years later, in 1956, *Time* magazine reported on a presentation he gave to city officials from Fort Worth about redevelopment of the congested downtown, where "parking space is inadequate and traffic motion slows to a crawl." The article stated that

> *civic leaders heard a Los Angeles and Manhattan community planner unveil a bold solution to their problem. They were advised to dig deep into the heart of their beloved Texas to create subterranean truck lanes, park every arriving automobile and turn streets within a downtown square mile into a pedestrian's paradise of shrubbery, statuary, malls, covered walks and sidewalk cafes...Author of the plan is Victor Gruen, who has pioneered some of the boldest new architectural projects in the country.*[33]

The article noted humorously:

> *When Gruen finished, his audience of Fort Worth community leaders enthusiastically appointed study committees. They were so impressed by the Texas-like immensity of the project that none stopped to chide him for an undiplomatic slip: his report had said that "Fort Worth now finds itself not keeping pace with Dallas."*[34]

This project would be the first of many Gruen proposals that sought to revitalize urban downtowns.

The offices of Gruen were an exciting place to work in the "Swinging Sixties" and were attracting a variety of young superstar architects. Among them was an upstart by the name of Frank Gehry. Although Gehry left the firm in 1960 because he felt he was not receiving his due promotions, he admitted in a recent interview with the *Architect's Newspaper* that being a junior associate was still an exhilarating experience:

> *I often got to work with Victor very closely, and with Rudy Baumfeld, and Edgardo Contini, people who I adored and respected...It was a place that was interested in art and culture and design...There was a lot of energy and it felt good. It was a very vibrant group and Rudy loved it, he loved all the younger people, as did Victor. They all used the energy of it, they loved the meetings and would have evening parties, inviting all of us.*

The offices of Victor Gruen Associates were an exhilarating place to work in the "Swinging Sixties," as Gruen was among the preeminent international commercial architects. *Image provided by Victor Gruen Collection, American Heritage Center, University of Wyoming. Used with permission.*

Gruen was not without his critics. Upon the construction of the suburban Southdale Shopping Center outside Minneapolis, Minnesota, widely credited to be the first completely enclosed shopping center in the world, Gruen's work was placed in the national spotlight. Shortly after Southland opened in 1956, it was visited by the legendary, and notoriously opinionated, Frank Lloyd Wright. The aging architect scoffed, "What is this, a railroad station or a bus station? In all this there should be increased freedom and graciousness. It is wholly lacking." Wright singled out a landscaped garden area and asked rhetorically, "Who wants to sit in this desolate looking spot? You've got a garden court that has all the evils of the village street and none of its charm." In a final lambasting, Wright complained, "You have tried to bring downtown out here. You should have left downtown downtown." The harshness of Wright's words was not lost on those who heard them. The title of the media piece that bore Wright's comments was "Minneapolis Crucified by Architect." Very likely, they were also not lost on Gruen.[35]

Gruen, while remembered for suburban malls and shopping centers, was most passionate about the work for which he is not remembered. Moreover, little of this work materialized. In Gruen's writings, his ultimate vision was for the revitalization of America's urban areas with structures like Randhurst. While smaller, newly growing cities—such as Kalamazoo, Michigan; Fresno, California; and Urbana, Illinois—adopted "Gruen Plans," the largest American cities appeared to lack interest.

So Gruen's suburban shopping centers were a gamble. By building these vast and beautiful centers, Gruen hoped to entice urban downtowns to follow suit. It was extremely likely that Gruen put so much of himself into Randhurst in order to entice the "powers that be" in nearby Chicago to allow him to redevelop State Street. It was probably also no coincidence that the three major retailers involved in Randhurst were also three very prominent State Street retailers.

Gruen was even asked about his feelings regarding the redevelopment of State Street and made no secret of his desire to do the project. *Chicago Daily News* reporter Tony Weitzel noted, in what proved to be quite a telling quip shortly after Randhurst opened:

> *Architect Victor Gruen took time out for little conversation after he wrapped his Randhurst shopping plaza shores* [sic]. *Randhurst, in case nobody noticed, is the world's largest shopping center of one roof. But it's destined to lose the title to a section of South Boston. That's where Gruen is blueprinting a State-Street-sized shopping center that will be completely under one roof, atmosphere-conditioned, and free of motor cars. After that, he'll build a similar project in London. In time, Gruen thinks, the cities of the world, at least in their central areas, will be independent of weather. What about our State St.? Gruen says he's ready anytime State St. is. Imagine 12 months of spring at State and Madison?*[36]

What, then, is Gruen's legacy? He was undoubtedly a paradoxical figure—a man who gave the automobile an unprecedented prominence in the daily life of Americans but personally despised the automobile and sought to banish it from urban downtowns, even going so far as to describe it as a "beast in need of domestication." He was a self-avowed socialist who has subsequently been dubbed the father of the shopping mall, perhaps the most prominent and conspicuous monument to the spoils of capitalism. It is likely that Gruen would be horrified by much of his own legacy, something he understood even in his own lifetime.

"We hope Randhurst will be an important milestone in the history of regional shopping centers in the United States." Victor Gruen (left) and George M. O'Neill, vice-president and general manager of Randhurst, examine a large-scale model of Randhurst, circa 1961.

Perhaps Gruen's biggest folly was that he did not understand, or grossly underestimated, the power of tax revenues and the desire for municipal services among suburban residents. As long as there were autonomous communities surrounding Randhurst that sought to attract residents and keep their tax dollars from escaping to the center, Randhurst would not remain the sole regional shopping center in the northwest suburbs for long.

Another Gruen legacy, which he also surely would have abhorred, is a psychological phenomenon known as the Gruen Transfer, or Gruen Effect. According to the website of a satirical Australian television show that bears the phenomenon's name:

> *The Gruen Transfer refers to the moment when we as consumers unwittingly respond to cues in the shopping environment that are designed to disorientate. Factors such as the lighting, sounds, temperature and the spatial arrangements of stores and displays interact, leading the customer to*

> *lose control of their critical decision making processes. Our eyes glaze over, our jaws slacken, we forget what we came for and become impulse buyers. So if you go into a mall to buy a mop and walk out with a toaster, a block of cheese and a badminton set, then the Gruen Transfer has probably played a role. Or maybe you just really like cheese.*[37]

Gruen would likely defend himself by claiming that many of these devices were designed to preserve the aesthetic integrity of his centers, as opposed to subconscious cues to buy with reckless abandon. While his legacy will undoubtedly continue to be scrutinized, either in celebration or damnation, Randhurst Shopping Center, for its part, was not only the "the height of Gruen's retailing dreams in suburbia," but it was also among Gruen's greatest self-actualizations. While many of Gruen's planned centers were scaled back by nervous investors who scoffed at the seemingly foolhardy notion of competing department stores located mere yards away from one another under one roof, Randhurst was continually, and lavishly, expanded.

Gruen made no secret of his hopes for Randhurst. He told a Chicago construction publication plainly, "We hope Randhurst will be an important milestone in the history of regional shopping centers in the United States." This statement held implications that Randhurst would serve as an important template not only for future shopping centers but also for *many* future shopping centers.[38]

Despite the fact that Gruen would have severely different attitudes regarding the shopping center later in his life, the construction of Randhurst would, in the meantime, captivate Chicagoland.

4

"This Most Unusual Shopping Center"

A Novel Groundbreaking Rite

On November 17, 1960, a Mount Prospect Fire Department tank truck raced to the Burmeister Farm with a fresh one-thousand-gallon water supply in a frenzied attempt to save a large barn that was built about the turn of the century. This fire, which was now burning out of control, had been started intentionally by officers of the Randhurst Corporation. However, this was by no means an act of arson, at least not in the criminal sense. Randhurst was committed to its image as an innovative and futuristic institution. As a result, it was determined to defy convention at every opportunity throughout the development, construction and operation of the shopping center.

The first of these opportunities occurred on this brisk November morning in 1960. With two hundred onlookers and the local and Chicago press corps and Mount Prospect Fire Department, under Chief Ed Haberkamp, dutifully looking on, officers of the Randhurst Corporation gathered for what was termed a "Barn-Burning Ceremony." The group was an impressive conglomerate of powerful Chicago retailers. They represented in body what Randhurst would represent in stone. They included James F. Tobin, president, and Werner Wieboldt, chairman, of Wieboldt's Department Stores, Inc; George M. O'Neill, vice-president and general manager of the Randhurst Corporation; Paul M. Hammaker, president of Montgomery Ward & Co.; and John T. Pirie Jr., of Carson, Pirie, Scott & Co., the mind behind the original plans for Randhurst.

The Randhurst Corporation elected George M. O'Neill as general manager and vice-president. He is seen here directing the busy construction site in the spring of 1961.

George M. O'Neill would serve as the public face of Randhurst throughout its inception and construction and made sure that the spectacular plans for Randhurst would not disappoint, all the while assuring concerned residents that Randhurst would be a good neighbor. O'Neill, who at the time of Randhurst's grand opening was thirty-nine years old, was a native of Charleston, North Carolina. The *Chicago Tribune* described him as "a respected leader in the shopping center community. O'Neill was one of the first trustees of the International Council of Shopping Centers." Previously, O'Neill had served as the Midwest regional manager for style forecaster Amos Parrish and as general manager of the nearby Harlem-Irving Shopping Center, completed in 1956, before being hired by the Randhurst Corporation in 1959.[39]

This spectacle was meant to replace the traditional groundbreaking ceremonies, and given the violence of the act, it was obviously designed to send a clear message about what Randhurst would mean with regard to things of the past. With the cameras flashing and the smartly clad Randhurst executives all smiles, a large match, placed by the group, ignited a small, sixty-year-old barn on the property. A puff of black smoke emerged from the barn and rose into the air, reportedly visible for miles around. The executives stood chuckling in front of the blazing structure. It

A Mount Prospect firefighter under the supervision of Chief Edwin Haberkamp (foreground) douses the large barn during the "Barn-Burning Ceremony," narrowly salvaging it.

served as quite a dramatic photo op, with the *Chicago Daily News* rhetorically asking in its caption, "Why are Wieboldt's Ward's [and] Carson's laughing at this fire?"[40]

However, in what could in many ways be seen as ironic, the fire quickly burned out of control. Near the small barn that was used for the photo op stood a larger barn that they were saving in order to house the massive earth-moving and construction equipment that would turn this pastoral farm into a cathedral of commerce. The Mount Prospect Fire Department rained a steady stream of water on the large barn to ensure its safety. Yet somehow, the flames from the small barn reached the larger one, and the fire department could not douse them. Then the water supply ran out. The tank truck was dispatched and hurried back to replenish the water. Fortunately, it arrived on time. The *Mount Prospect Herald* reported:

> *While the firemen and the chief told spectators before the ceremony that they could "bet" on their saving the adjoining barn, they were beginning to take odds among themselves that the construction companies would have to plan to build themselves another storage shed.*[41]

This episode proved to be, quite literally, a baptism by fire for Randhurst. In concurrence with Gruen's vision, Randhurst would be unapologetically massive and would on numerous occasions command attention in a theatrical fashion. Now that the old Burmeister Farm had been spectacularly laid to rest, the earth around it began to come to life.

According to a company publication entitled *Randhurst Facts*, the materials that would go into Randhurst were impressive, even by contemporary standards. It is telling that the company would go to such lengths as to publish a prospectus discussing the sheer size and materials put into Randhurst, as if these accomplishments were not impressive in and of themselves.

The list of materials that went into Randhurst was certainly extraordinary, and the company did not hide this fact. Among the resources that went into the building were 6,400 tons of steel; 65 tons of sheet metal; 307,000 yards of site-stripping and excavation; 23,000 cubic yards of building backfill; 1,915,500 lineal feet of electrical wire and cable; 440,500 linear feet of conduit; 803,600 bricks; 376,400 concrete blocks; 50,600 glazed tile; 40,500 paving bricks; 35 tons of building stone; 26,400 feet of sewer and water pipe; 500,000 square feet of acoustical tile; 7,500 lighting fixtures; 50,000 linear feet of curbs and gutters; and 534 plumbing fixtures.

The pamphlet also listed the official start date of construction of Randhurst as December 5, 1960. There were no winters off. Workers bore through the mud and snow throughout the winter of 1961, laying the massive triangular foundation for the building. Amazingly, the massive building was finished ahead of schedule in the late summer of 1962. In just over a year and a half, two million man hours of work were reported.

By the time of its construction, the plans for Randhurst had grown even larger than proposed. In order to attract the proper caliber and number of tenants, Randhurst had to look good on the "drawing board" before it was actually constructed. Various architectural renderings of the futuristic building were commissioned, the most dramatic of which were executed by illustrator Carlos Diniz. Diniz was an innovator in the field of architectural illustration. He

This panoramic rendering of the Galleria at Randhurst, circa 1961, was sketched by Carlos Diniz. He was an innovator in architectural illustrating. He also conceptualized the World Trade Center during this period.

began his career with Victor Gruen in 1952, until, with Gruen's encouragement, he established his own studio in 1957. About the time that Diniz completed his panoramic sketches of Randhurst, he caught the eye of architect Minoru Yamasaki, who invited him to contribute to an exciting new project in which Yamasaki was submitting a proposal: the World Trade Center in New York City. As Diniz recalled, "Yamasaki showed me a model so tall it pierced the ceiling of his studio and left me agog. How to make this project look right in scale with its surroundings was only one of the problems." Diniz was able to accomplish this, however, and the contract was awarded to Yamasaki's firm. The resulting fame catapulted Diniz into preeminence, and his firm became the leading illustrator for the building boom of the 1970s and '80s. Diniz passed away in 2001, less than two months before Yamasaki's soaring twin towers were completely destroyed by Islamic fundamentalists in the attacks of September 11.[42]

Promotion of Randhurst was also assisted by a large-scale model of the center. Like the plans for Randhurst itself, the model was quite impressive. The model was able to be opened down the center, which revealed the various levels. The model was also wired with electricity to show off its dramatic lighting effects. Photographs of the model were used often in promotion of the center.

Given the alliance of the three retailers, a triangular design would now characterize the building. The theme of the triangle would define the image

An impressive Randhurst scale model is examined by O'Neill and an unidentified man. Presumably, it is Karl O. Van Leuven Jr., Gruen Associates partner in charge of Randhurst.

of Randhurst, and in addition to the construction of the building itself, it would be used in almost every facet of Randhurst, from the layout of the polished concrete floors and planters to the design of the company's logo. *Randhurst Facts* described the design as "unique and exciting" and glowingly stated, "The center is in the shape of a huge triangle, with the three department stores situated at the points of the triangle. Since Randhurst is entirely under one roof, shoppers and tenants alike will spend less time walking between points within the center. Walking distance between stores is considerably shorter than in centers much smaller than Randhurst."

While it was already significantly shortened, walking, at least vertically, was assisted by the installation of twelve state-of-the-art, high-capacity escalators installed by the Otis Elevator Company. The company proudly

Unique Christmas Display!
Available for your store in 1964
ON EXHIBIT NOW AT RANDHURST
Christmas
SPECTACULAR!
Eleven custom-built, fully animated and movable display windows depicting "The Dolls' Christmas." Viewed by hundreds-of-thousands of people at Randhurst, now for sale as a complete unit. Usable as free-standing units or as window displays. For detailed description, dimensions, price, etc., phone, wire or write: Robert J. Flynn, General Manager, Randhurst Corp., 999 Elmhurst Road, Mt. Prospect, Illinois, 259-0500 (Area Code 312).
ELEVEN SCENES—
ANIMATED—
FULLY PORTABLE
World's Largest Shopping Center...All Under One Roof
R
RANDHURST
999 Elmhurst Road—Mt. Prospect, Illinois

Randhurst was certainly respected among trade publications, so much so that even its used Christmas decorations were a status symbol, as this period advertisement implies. *Image courtesy of Dave Aldrich.*

used its involvement at Randhurst as something of a status symbol, boasting in a press release, "The three department stores will each have four escalators. Two between the main and upper levels, and two between the main and concourse levels. Each escalator is four feet wide, large enough for two people to ride comfortably side by side and able to carry 8,000 persons an hour." Otis was not alone. Dozens of trades used some variation of the tagline "Chosen at Randhurst" in their advertising.[43]

The efficiency built into the triangular structure was also a point of pride for the company. It bragged that operations required a minimum number of employees and that its approximately fifty workers, from executives and engineers to maintenance and security personnel, were a model of efficiency for the world's largest shopping center under one roof.

Architectural Forum took notice of this design and in a 1962 article dubbed Randhurst a "big pinwheel on the prairie" and praised Gruen's design process for the layout:

> *The intensive use of galleria space evolved directly from the problem of tying together three large stores of about equal size. Gruen at first conceived*

Amazingly, construction of Randhurst began in the winter of 1960–1. The crew worked through the mud and snow to lay the foundation for the triangular footprint of the building, seen in this aerial photo taken in early 1961.

a simple triangular pattern, but this left too much space in the central court. On the other hand, had the central court area been too greatly reduced, the passages reaching from the core to the large stores would have become too long, narrow and generally unattractive. Also, a straight triangle would not have drawn shoppers so effectively as does the pinwheel.[44]

The 108-acre site of Randhurst would now center on this great triangle, which occupied over 10 acres of the site. The interior of the great building contained 1.25 million square feet of space. Each department store averaged nearly 200,000 square feet. As per Gruen's recommendations, the space would not only contain retail space but also public spaces, offices and a large community meeting room.

Sixty acres would be set aside for parking. As previously mentioned, given that the automobile was vital, parking would be essential to Randhurst's success. Parking for as many as ten thousand cars was constructed. Each segment of the parking lot was designated by color and pictorial representations, initially using various types of fruit. The company boasted that the parking lanes were clearly marked and would guide motorists to extra-wide stalls, at a fifty-five-degree angle, that could be driven into with

Randhurst's massive lots were illuminated by scattered thirty-foot, six-pronged lighting trees. The parking areas were given fruit designations, in this case, Wieboldt's "Grape Lot."

one turn of the wheel. The parking area was also outfitted with ninety thirty-foot light towers, each of which contained six three-hundred-watt incandescent lighting fixtures. Randhurst Corporation claimed that the illumination provided a "bright, safe parking area without harsh, offending glare."

The remaining thirty acres were set aside for landscaped areas. Randhurst's massive parking lot was adorned with fifty-eight parking lot planting islands, containing 453 trees, 225 plants, four thousand square feet of sod and seventy-five hundred pounds of grass seed. The landscape architecture was meticulously planned by Franz Lipp. Elements of nature were extremely important to the aesthetics of Randhurst, both inside and out. In addition to the exterior landscaping, there were a variety of plants, trees and flowers inside the building. In one of Randhurst's first press releases, it was announced: "[Randhurst] will be the largest regional shopping center in the country, and will be completely covered, yet will have an outdoor effect."[45] In a letter to Mount Prospect residents from George M. O'Neill shortly before Randhurst's opening, he took the opportunity to brag about the building's exotic plant life. In addition to vegetation, there were also a number of other aesthetic features, designed to invoke the sublimity of nature, that would adorn the center.

The massive job of supplying water to Randhurst was accomplished by a 150-foot water tower. On the first Friday evening of 1961, General Manager O'Neill, Randhurst attorney Ned Saunders, Victor Gruen Associates representative Roy Brinker and President Harold Spurway again appeared before the village zoning board to petition for construction of the water tower. They detailed the work involved in choosing the location of the tower and told the board that the tower would be of a modern style, unlike the old-style conventional towers. The decorative style of the tower, though quite common today, was cutting edge in January 1961. It was then commonly referred to as a "giant golf ball"–type structure. The petitioners stated that the 150-foot height was necessary to gain needed pressure for fire prevention. Because the village did not anticipate the probability of such a lofty structure within its limits, a special variation of an 85-foot-building-height permit for the center had to be granted. The Randhurst representatives also stated that Well #6, specially designed for the property, was nearing completion. The property for the well had previously been deeded to the village by the Randhurst Corporation.

The landmark water tower, which still stands today, was located on the southwest corner of the property. The 150,000-gallon tower was used for the center's plumbing needs, in addition to providing fire protection and

"A new landmark for these suburbs." Randhurst's 150-foot water tower is seen nearing completion in this construction photo. It still stands today.

sustaining the landscaping. Upon its construction, it was declared "a new landmark for these suburbs" and painted white, with Randhurst's distinctive triangular logo illuminated at night to serve as a "guiding light" to those from the area not familiar with the location.[46]

In what was perhaps a defensive move to assure Mount Prospect citizens that their tax dollars were not funding the building outright, the Randhurst Corporation reported that a ten-inch water main linking the building to Mount Prospect's water system was planned, contracted and paid for by the corporation. At a village board meeting, O'Neill quelled any doubt that the Village of Mount Prospect would be funding Randhurst's water needs by presenting a check in the amount of $6,000, the "promised amount," to connect Randhurst's water main to village Well #6.[47] It was then turned over to Mount Prospect to become village property, after which Randhurst purchased its water from the village at regular commercial rates. The water was then treated by Randhurst's own water-softening system.

It was also reported that the water tower had another unintended feature. At the time, the tower would have been the tallest structure in the area and thus was used as a beacon by airline pilots. When nearby O'Hare Airport started serving commercial jets in the early 1960s, pilots had difficulty navigating through the northwest suburbs. The newly built Randhurst served as their signpost. They often needed to locate the water tower for their landings. "I remember talking to pilots who used it as a frequent landmark," recalled one

Randhurst official, Marketing Director John Lehrer. "They looked for the dome and the water tower on landings."[48]

John Lehrer was an early marketing consultant for the booming business of shopping centers. While his offices were located in Milwaukee, he was personally contacted by O'Neill and asked if he would consider working for Randhurst. Lehrer was so impressed by the spectacle of the Barn-Burning Ceremony that he agreed and moved his operations to Randhurst, then his second client.[49]

In another convention-defying event, Randhurst marked its completion of construction with the same spectacle that began it. In a play on a cornerstone-laying ceremony, the company held a "domestone"-laying ceremony. The dome was the literal and figurative center of Randhurst, weighing two hundred tons and rising almost seventy feet above the floor. At a luncheon held on March 1, 1962, company officers, tenants, elected officials and the press corps yet again gathered at the site of the massive building, which was now just months away from completion.

Just prior to this ceremony, the giant boilers used to regulate the constant seventy-two-degree temperature at Randhurst were turned on. Unlike the Barn-Burning Ceremony a year and a half prior, this ceremony went off without a hitch. O'Neill proudly proclaimed:

> *When the boilers were fired, the heating system easily met every requirement. And with the heat on we are able to move ahead with other construction. Randhurst's heating system is immense as it would have to be to serve a structure so large. But heating is only half the task of the system. The thousands of feet of ductwork and pipe that heat the center in winter will also cool it in the summer.*

The gargantuan climate-control system, one of the first attempted on such a grand scale, was designed by Robert E. Hattis Engineers, Inc., of Skokie, Illinois. The heating portion consisted of three massive hot water boilers and two six-hundred-horsepower steam boilers. The *Mount Prospect Herald* reported that "the two steam boilers are larger than an automobile and the three hot water boilers approach the size of a steam engine."[50] The system was capable of delivering twenty-five thousand gallons of hot water to Randhurst's tenants, in addition to heating two thousand gallons of fuel oil for the boilers each day. Sixty thousand gallons of oil for the boilers were stored in two underground tanks. The fuel supply was never allowed to fall below ten thousand gallons, to keep Randhurst comfortable and protected in the event

Randhurst's massive boilers are lifted into place with the assistance of a crane in the summer of 1961.

of a weather emergency. Additional water was heated to two hundred degrees and sent through pressure to all areas of Randhurst. The cooling system contained capacity of forty-two hundred tons of refrigeration. Chilled water was pumped into the center at forty-five degrees and was returned through the ductwork at sixty-five degrees.

The climate-control system was truly an impressive feat. The heated and chilled water was pumped to coils located throughout the structure, where fans dispersed the air to "a web of ducts to hundreds of outlets throughout the center." It was able to circulate 700,000 cubic feet of air per minute in order to maintain the highly publicized "72 degrees year round" temperature. O'Neill boasted:

> *The system will provide anything we want in the way of climate control. Randhurst will be as comfortable as a fireside in winter and as refreshing as a lake shore in the summer. Should the unstable spring and fall weather require it, we can mix the heating and cooling to meet whatever conditions exist. The Randhurst heating system has the capacity to heat 2,000 homes.*

The heating system used a "whopping" amount of fuel with "tar-like consistency" to accomplish this—as much as fifteen to sixteen hundred gallons daily when the temperatures were near freezing, and as much as three thousand gallons when the weather conditions dropped below freezing.[51] In

Randhurst's impressive physical plant was charged with the task of maintaining the much-touted "72 degrees year round." The large boilers can be seen in the upper right of this picture.

addition to housing the immense heating system, Randhurst's lower level would offer other features, ranging from the practical to the paranoid.

The domestone laying, or rather hoisting, climaxed in the raising of a time capsule to the dome. In front of the dozens of attendees decked out in fine suits and donning ceremonial hardhats, O'Neill, Tobin, J.P. Hansen representing The Fair store and Virgil Hansen of Carson, Pirie, Scott & Co. smiled for another memorable photo op in which the four men lifted a gleaming copper box engraved with the words "Randhurst Center" to the rafters of the newly completed dome. The time capsule contained a number of items commemorating the occasion, reported the *Mount Prospect Herald*. Among these items was a copy of Mount Prospect mayor Clarence "C.O" Schlaver's eloquent speech welcoming Randhurst to the community, in which he stated:

> *March 1, 1962. On this day, the Village of Mount Prospect, Illinois, recognizes an event of Municipal importance—the "domestone" ceremony of Randhurst Corporation. This is a construction and progress milestone in the building of a shopping facility which the official family of Mount Prospect recognizes is destined to become a new "city" within our corporate limits. Today we have seen in mortar and stone, in steel and aluminum, what men of vision and financial resources have wrought in order to build a center of shops, offices and services which will serve thousands of homeowners in an area reaching from Chicago to the Wisconsin line. This is a center which today stands unique as a structure under one roof, centrally air-conditioned*

George M. O'Neill hoists the Randhurst time capsule to the rafters of the dome. As of the close of 2010, the capsule is still missing, and its full contents are unknown.

and with joint servicing of utilities. It is designed to make shopping easier, parking more convenient. It reflects the astute planning of Victor Gruen Associates and the developers in order that these advantages lead to better merchandising. The Village of Mount Prospect welcomes this new "city" established at its present northern borders. This welcome is extended with full consciousness of the impact this will have through tax revenue, making possible the extension of municipal services for the benefit of all residents of Mount Prospect. We extend official congratulations to both the officials of Randhurst Corporation and those firms who will become tenants of the shopping center. We also voice our sincere thanks to those connected with its construction, for they have cooperated well in following our ordinances. It is our wish that the Randhurst Shopping Center will fulfill all of the dreams of those who have been a part of converting the cornfields of yesterday into the merchandising realities of tomorrow.[52]

Representatives of the department stores also placed copies of their remarks in the capsule. Also, a complete set of Randhurst's blueprints was placed in the container. The *Herald* reported that a *Chicago Tribune* reporter bid one dollar for a surprise package item, which was considered Randhurst's first sale, and the dollar bill was also placed in the capsule. Robert Y. Paddock of Paddock Publications placed a copy of the March 1 *Mount Prospect Herald* into the box, in addition to other newspapers, probably the *Chicago Tribune*, *Daily News* or the *Sun-Times*. To date, the time capsule has not been found.

By the completion of the ceremony, Randhurst was now bigger than ever, touted by local papers as "the only planned center in the nation with three complete and competing department stores…which will also include 100 other shops and services as well as 50 professional office suites." The newspaper also noted that Randhurst was "the largest building of its kind in the world." O'Neill reported on the occasion of the domestone ceremony that

> *Randhurst general construction is now 85 percent complete and is running about five percent ahead of schedule. Presently many of the walls for the stores and shops are going up, plumbing and electrical facilities are being completed, plastering has begun, and ceilings are being installed.*

The Randhurst Corporation undoubtedly wanted the shopping center to be a place of activity and excitement. This apparently was the case even before the center was opened. As *Mount Prospect Herald* reporter Melda Lynn (who was also dubbed "the first woman visitor" at Randhurst) proved, even

Left to right: George M. O'Neill, Construction Project Manager Donald Littrell and *Mount Prospect Herald* reporter and "first woman visitor" Melda Lynn at the site. Lynn was arguably Randhurst's biggest booster in the local media.

the construction of the center proved to be a breathtaking sight. After a tour of the construction in early August 1961, she wrote:

> *What does it take to build Randhurst, the world's largest regional shopping center? More than 1,000 yards of concrete each day to build foundations, underground truck passages, floors and wall (150 truck loads); tons of steel and wood; two 180-ft. booms on 100 ton cranes; hundreds of pieces of earth moving equipment; millions of bricks; miles of electric wiring; and of course, thousands of skilled laborers, surveyors, engineers and architects. These facts were discovered by Melda Lynn of Paddock Publications, first woman to tour the 110-acre construction site. Through mud, around trucks, up and down platforms, and underground, the tour revealed a beehive of activity in every corner of the area which will eventually be the world's largest shopping center under one roof, containing 1,200,000 sq. ft. of floor space. Randhurst is 30 per cent completed, which is "right on the construction schedule nose," states George M. O'Neill, general manager of Randhurst. Construction of the dome, which will be the focal point over a large galleria, will be started within a few days. The entire center is expected to be under roof by November 1. One of the most interesting activities, is the conveying of 1,000 yards of concrete, brought in by 150 trucks each day to the various places where it is to be used. The trucks dump the concrete into large conveyers. Laborers fill over-sized wheelbarrows from the conveyors and "run," not walk, to the place where it is to be dumped. A constant stream of manpower used in the cement portion of the construction makes a sharp contrast to the huge machinery used for other phases of the construction. Really, a magnificent sight to watch is the large crane lifting a huge steel beam up over the different levels and into the guiding arms of the steelworkers. It takes complete concentration and coordination between the operator of the crane and the steelworker precariously perched on top of the highest beam. Large pieces of machinery are carried through the air by the crane, as though they were toys strung on a string, from one level to another. Automatic packers, pieces of machinery which pack the earth into a more solid form, are used by men down in the lower levels of the center where truck tunnels are being installed. Regardless of the amount of machinery, or the type of work it does, it still takes manpower to work it, guide it and keep it in running order. The manpower, it is obvious, is still "king" in the construction of the huge center. Fifteen miles of double lane paving is now being put in for the parking lot to provide space for 10,000 cars. A crew of approximately 600 men comprise a weekly payroll from $80,000 to*

The superstructure of Randhurst begins to take shape as the frame of the dome rises into the air in September 1961.

> *$100,000. When the center is under roof, construction of the 90 specialty shops and three main department stores will begin. Three major department stores will form the apexes of the triangular shaped center, located at the northeast corner of Rand and Elmhurst rds., in Mount Prospect. These will be occupied by Carson Pirie Scott, Wieboldt's and The Fair. Leases for 14 specialty shops have already been contracted for, bringing the total space now contracted for to 684,858 sq. ft...In the meantime, things shaping up from the mortar, brick and mud of today will emerge into a shopping center unequalled in beauty and convenience—one eagerly awaited by thousands of anxious shoppers from the northwest suburban area.*[53]

Lynn also reported that women were involved in the process of building Randhurst. In a special section of the *Mount Prospect Herald*, she reported colorfully, but admiringly, on the roles these women were playing: "Behind every success—whether a single man or a giant project such as the $20 million Randhurst Shopping Center—There's bound to be a woman in the background." Lynn profiled Anna Mae O'Malley, "a little Irish gal," secretary to George M. O'Neill, who was

> *hired even before he was hired or before a desk for her first office in Chicago arrived. She speaks enthusiastically about her work—and what woman wouldn't who had the joyous task of writing checks from a bank account that literally holds millions of dollars! While her shopping includes steel, concrete blocks, and other "staples," she writes the checks to pay for the*

It took a small army to build Randhurst, as seen in this photo depicting the "shack" that temporarily housed the company's offices during construction, as well as the cars that brought hundreds of workers to the construction site.

> *items with the same conscientiousness of a housewife paying for the weekly supply of groceries.*

The piece also described registered nurse Betty Bridges, who was responsible for administering first aid to the workers. Her duties of "routine nature" were described as "dispensing hangover pills, ulcer pills, tranquilizers (on doctors orders) to bandaging cut fingers or cleaning infected hangnails." Bridges also worked closely with civil engineer Thad Bryant to identify and prevent safety hazards. The newspaper noted that "the only problem they haven't been able to solve is how to keep workers from being so astonished when they see a woman around the project they are apt to drop a brick on their toes or smash their fingers with a hammer."[54]

While overall the safety record at Randhurst appeared to be exceptional, the construction site could certainly be perilous. Bridges recalled an instance when she had to climb to the top of the dome to administer first aid during a forty-two-mile-per-hour gale. There were documented instances of serious injuries. Bridges had to rush construction worker Gino Pelligrina to nearby Northwest Community Hospital under police escort after he fell two stories. Immediately afterward, the newspapers listed him in "fair" condition. Another construction worker, Libero

Randhurst Shopping Center nears completion in this aerial photo, circa 1962.

Santucci, was caught in the cave-in of a trench bank but, amazingly, escaped unharmed.[55] Tragically, one worker, Joseph Garrity, was killed after a fall from a scaffold shortly before the grand opening.[56]

Clearly, the massive human effort was such that Randhurst could not be realized without it. The labors of thousands of men and women made it possible, from the highest-ranking State Street official to the painstaking construction workers. As Randhurst neared completion, plans commenced to properly welcome it to the Chicago area, using all the pomp, splendor and spectacle that had come to define it.

5

"This Is Randhurst"

Dear Neighbor:

Because you live close to Randhurst, and because we'll be neighbors for a long time to come, I thought it would be a good idea to give you some of the facts and details about this truly fantastic shopping center.

In this first Randhurst Report, you'll learn something about the construction of Randhurst and what its physical facilities will offer. In succeeding reports, we'll tell you about the stores and shops you'll find at Randhurst and about Randhurst's Grand Opening Plans. Our Grand Opening will be Thursday, August 16th.

First of all, Randhurst represents an entirely new concept in shopping centers. Designed by the renowned architect Victor Gruen, Randhurst is the largest enclosed-mall shopping center. Yes, all of Randhurst's 1,200,000 square feet of space is under one roof...and completely climate-controlled to maintain a comfortable seventy-two-degree temperature year 'round.

Randhurst is located on 100 acres of land at the intersection of Rand and Elmhurst Roads in Mount Prospect, Illinois. It is bounded on the south by Foundry and on the north by Euclid Avenue.

Randhurst has parking facilities for over 7,500 cars in extra-wide, well-lighted parking stalls located close to the store.

The triangular layout of Randhurst makes it possible to feature three famous full-line department stores, one at each point of the triangle. Because of this unique layout, walking distance between stores is kept to a minimum.

And speaking of stores…in addition to Carson, Pirie, Scott & Co., Wieboldt's and The Fair…you'll find many of your other favorite stores at Randhurst too. There are many of America's finest stores, shops, restaurants and services, virtually an entire city, all under one roof.

There are loads of other wonderful features for your convenience and pleasure at Randhurst, for example: Your club or group can enjoy complete auditorium and meeting room facilities, including food service.

And if you like true beauty in your shopping atmosphere, you'll want to see the many special fountains and sculptures by some of America's finest artists, displayed in Randhurst's malls. There are beautiful trees and planters that grow year 'round at Randhurst, bringing their natural beauty indoors. You'll also find vast varieties of exotic flowers, surrounded by comfortable benches where you can relax while shopping.

This is our first report to you on Randhurst…the world's largest shopping center all under one roof. We know you'll want to see Randhurst for yourself just as soon as it's ready on August 16th. Once you do, you'll want to come back again and again…to spend an entire day in this most unusual shopping center…Randhurst…all under one roof.

I'll be looking forward to seeing you soon.

Cordially,
RANDHURST CORPORATION
George M. O'Neill
Vice President and General Manager[57]

The immediate days leading up to the grand opening of Randhurst Shopping Center were electric and had the entire Chicagoland area buzzing, so much so that it caused *Mount Prospect Herald* editor Stuart Paddock to proclaim in his column, "We have never met so many Brother Editors in one room as we did on Monday noon when Randhurst held a press preview of the new shopping center. There was not a Chicago daily or weekly newspaper in the area which was not represented."

Certainly, Randhurst knew the power of newspapers. Before the doors to the center even opened, Randhurst had set a promotional record, in addition to its physical records, with what was billed as the largest special advertising section ever published in the *Chicago Daily Tribune*—a fifty-page advertisement sent to over 200,000 households. The newspaper further noted that Randhurst had concentrated 76 percent of its total promotional budget with the *Tribune*.[58] Interestingly, it appears that Randhurst, with all its aspirations toward the future, did little to no advertising on the still new-fangled television.

Various charitable preview celebrations were also held in the days before Randhurst opened to the public. Among the first groups to see the dazzling new shopping center was the Mount Prospect Infant Welfare Society, at a black-tie event that would inadvertently reveal one of the shopping center's hidden treasures: an opulent women's bathroom. The event was held on Saturday, August 11, five days before the center opened its doors to the public. Mrs. W.C. Elbracht announced to the *Tribune* that the gala evening would feature a seven-course dinner under the dome and a fashion show, where the sponsoring three major department stores would show off their fall wares.[59] "No one word could possibly describe [it]," reported Melda Lynn, ever the Randhurst booster. She proclaimed it "a lavish affair, probably the biggest event of the Mount Prospect Social Season." She continued with fawning detail:

> *The black tie event* [began] *with champagne followed by filet mignon and other gourmet food. Cooked according to extra special recipes. Then came petits fours. Most guests believing this was a wonderful end to a perfect dinner were delighted by an "encore" provided when waiters descended from the stairways of the terrace level leading into Carson's Floating Pavilion restaurant bearing silver trays of flaming baked Alaska.*

The subsequent "Focus on Fashion" show featured fifty-three outfits under varying categories, including: "Fall in a Blaze of Red Glory," "The Casual Elegant Look," "The Costume Takes Precedence," "The Shapes of Fashion," "Enchanted Evenings" and "The Elegance of Fur." Lynn concluded that this splendid evening had occurred in "the most colorful, unbelievable center ever imagined."[60]

A small battalion of "Randhurst Girls" was sent out to go door-to-door throughout Mount Prospect and the surrounding communities to distribute personal invitations to the grand-opening celebrations. The fourteen girls—eleven residents of Mount Prospect and three from Arlington Heights—were to "add a colorful note to the already beautiful center with their costumes designed in the Randhurst colors of yellow, green and orange." These young women also acted as official hostesses for the center throughout its grand-opening ceremony.

While the Randhurst Girls pounded the pavement, the center was a beehive of painters, tradesmen, landscapers and various other workers frantically putting the finishing touches on the building for its big debut. The level of detail was such that one impressed Chicago newspaper reported:

The "Randhurst Girl" at left is Darlene Preski. The other women in the photo, as well as the shy child in the lower right corner, are unidentified.

> *Workers clad in swim suits readjusted misbehaving fountains as the Randhurst Shopping Center in Mount Prospect prepared for its Thursday grand opening. The splashing workers were just a few among hundreds putting the finishing touches on the $21,000,000 shopping plaza, which embodies revolutionary principles of design and marketing.*[61]

Reporter Melda Lynn, who had covered Randhurst almost since its inception, wrote about the palpable excitement on the front page of the *Mount Prospect Herald* on Thursday, August 16, 1962, stating simply what virtually everyone in the northwest suburbs was thinking:

> *Randhurst opens today. Finally arrived is the day all Mount Prospect has been waiting for since May 13, 1959, when it was first announced that this village had been chosen as the best location in the Chicagoland area for building the multi-million dollar shopping facility. Randhurst is the largest regional shopping center in the United States. What's more, it's the largest center under one roof in the entire world. Mount Prospect residents*

have already begun to reap many benefits from this gigantic $21 million enterprise, created and sponsored by three of the best known and respected department stores in the country.

On this picturesque late summer morning, the newly claimed northern border of the Village of Mount Prospect was perhaps the most festive place in the northwest suburbs, if not the entire Chicagoland area. At 9:00 a.m., village officials, officers of the Randhurst Corporation and the famed architect Victor Gruen himself marched in a parade, the largest yet in Mount Prospect's history, thrown to commemorate the day when Randhurst's doors were finally opened to the public. Representing the regional impact that the opening of the structure would have, elected officials from the nearby communities of Park Ridge, Des Plaines, Wheeling, Arlington Heights, Rolling Meadows, Palatine and others also participated in the parade. Seven marching bands took part in the march to Randhurst, including the famed Chicago bagpipe troupe the Stock Yard Kilty Band. The "noisy and colorful" debut of Randhurst was covered extensively by the Chicago media and was the culmination of almost four years of effort. At a luncheon during the day's festivities, the pomp and circumstance deeply impressed a spokesman from the International Council of Shopping Centers. Albert Sussman, executive

Aerial view of Randhurst during the days of the grand opening, 1962.

secretary to the council, was heard to remark, "Randhurst need take a back seat to no one."

The influx of the thousands who attended the grand opening from all over Chicagoland were led to Randhurst by a special detail of the Mount Prospect Police, who efficiently guided traffic through improved thoroughfares. Elmhurst Road had been widened to four lanes from Rand Road to Palatine Road to accommodate the traffic that Randhurst was expected to draw. Euclid, Rand and Foundry Roads received new pavement and additional widening near the center.[62] The entire road project around Randhurst was referred to as a "junior expressway." The Randhurst Corporation presented a check for $200,000 to the Cook County Board of Commissioners to assist in offsetting the cost of this nearly $1.5 million project.[63] For those who could not drive to the center, travel arrangements were made by a special agreement between the Chicago & Northwestern Railroad and the United Motor Coach Company, where a special shuttle would run to Randhurst from the Mount Prospect train station at the cost of twenty-five cents each way. As an additional mark of efficiency, it was announced that the commuter trains would arrive eleven minutes after the hour, while the buses would depart a prompt fifteen minutes after the hour.[64]

The festivities were marked by six ribbon-cutting ceremonies, one for each of Randhurst's arcade entrances. The first ribbon was cut by twelve-year-old Diane Hahnfield. Miss Hahnfield was the granddaughter of the Burmeisters, who had sold the majority of the land to the Randhurst Corporation years earlier. The event was a full-circle moment. Cheers arose as Diane opened this space-age monument that marked the remains of her family's farm. The additional ribbons were cut by Mayor Schlaver; C. Virgil Martin; J.P. Hansen, president of The Fair; James F. Tobin; and, of course, George M. O'Neill. Schlaver proudly stated:

> *This historic day was predicted two years ago, and has come to pass on this 16th day of August, 1962, just as the men of rare planning, merchandising, financing, and construction ability predicted. Of all the wonders of this magnificent center, I think that meeting the predicted completion time is perhaps the most important.*[65]

As O'Neill and other officials spoke, officials from the three department stores dropped three keys into a propane-fueled melting device, where they were melted into one key, symbolizing the strength that Randhurst would have through the unity of these powerful retailers.

An unidentified dignitary, presumably a representative of one of the three department stores, symbolically melts a key as Marketing Director John Lehrer speaks.

Shortly afterward, ten thousand balloons were released into the air. While this event was visually stunning, it served a dual purpose, which was, as always, tied in to the promotion of the shopping center. In an event that would likely not be allowed today, each balloon contained a small colored key. When the balloon inevitably popped, the key fell to the earth. The keys, when found, were to be taken to the center and inserted into three large treasure chests, which contained various prizes. Keys were also mailed throughout the northwest region and handed out to patrons as they entered the center during the grand-opening festivities. The *Randhurster* reported that this unique key promotion, which was referred to as "Key-Motion," also ensured repeat business. The keys were four different colors, one for each week of September. Keys were to be redeemed each week of September, according to color. In the weeks of September following the grand opening, people drove in from as far away as Rockford and Kenosha, Wisconsin, for a chance to unlock a chest.[66] The prizes ranged from "a set of automobile tires to a portable phonograph to a men's wardrobe of shirts."[67]

As a Dixieland band struck up "When the Saints Go Marching In," thousands of shoppers jammed into the center's arcades. They were greeted by rows of lockers: "turquoise, olive and orange are among the bright colors of the built-in steel compartments." Surely, many noticed that they would be able to store their coats, hats, boots and bundles as the winter months quickly descended on Chicago.[68] The music and many announcements throughout the day were heard by all through the assistance of over one thousand hi-fi speakers placed throughout the center. Additionally, strategically placed

This magnificent panoramic view of Randhurst's interior graced a postcard shortly after the center's opening. *Image courtesy of Dave Aldrich.*

microphone jacks assisted in the varying promotions that the center would employ. When not used for promotions or paging, guests were treated to pleasant background music, courtesy of the company widely credited with (or blamed for) the creation of "elevator music," Muzak Corporation. Muzak, like Otis elevators, used Randhurst as a status symbol, utilizing a full-color advertisement of it in trade publications.[69]

The climax of the grand-opening events occurred under the massive two-hundred-ton dome of the structure, which was given the elegant moniker of "the Galleria" and would serve as the aforementioned "monumental landmark" required of Gruen's shopping centers. Colorful beams of late summer sunlight pierced through the stained-glass figures ringing the clerestory windows underneath the dome. The company described it as

> *the center of attraction, as well as the center of Randhurst's physical structure...a magnificently domed central plaza consisting of four levels. The Dome itself is 64 feet high and is estimated to weigh in excess of 200 tons. Its design allows for maximum sunlight to filter through to the central area below.*

The Galleria was divided into four levels, each of which served as a representation of the varying roles, in addition to commerce, that

Randhurst would play in the community. The highest level, known as the Terrace, surrounded the dome and was home to professional offices, including medical and dental. Offices of governmental agencies would also make their home in this area.

The Pavilion, which could easily be thought of as the hub of the wheel to Randhurst, featured a spacious restaurant, cocktail lounge and coffee shop. A section of the Pavilion located directly underneath the dome itself was set aside for promotional and community events, such as fashion shows, arts and crafts exhibits and concerts. There was an interesting focal point of the Galleria, the design of which was so revolutionary that it was featured on the cover of *Shopping Center Age* in February 1962. O'Neill playfully remarked to the magazine that "we will practice a bit of levitation," as the publication billed the Pavilion as a "floating restaurant" that contained no sidewalls or partitions. The aptly named Tree Top Restaurant was accompanied, naturally, by the Bird's Nest Cocktail Lounge. The company stated, "While customers dine, they can enjoy the fountains, gardens and sculpture harmoniously blended in the Randhurst décor." The center was also home to the Apple Basket Restaurant and Pancake Shop, "for more informal dining"; the Randhurst Corned Beef Center, "with the flavor of an old coach house"; and the "Parisian atmosphere" of La Petit Café and Le Rendezvous. All of the center's food service was operated solely by Carson's, which was also the exclusive food vendor at nearby O'Hare Airport.[70]

The Galleria, under the dome in the center of Randhurst, was home to the "floating" Tree Top Restaurant on the Pavilion level, with the Bazaar level immediately beneath.

The "festive and colorful" Bazaar level immediately below contained lazy stairways and led to red brick paths surrounding open shops, flanked by large planters with tropical foliage. The lowest and final level of the Galleria was the Concourse. This level was home to the numerous service shops located in Randhurst. By the time of its opening, the center contained a beauty shop, barbershop, cleaner's, tailor's and shoe shop. It was also home to the popular wormwood-paneled Tartan Tray Cafeteria. In accordance with its role as a center of community life, various meeting rooms were located in the Concourse, including the Town Hall. The Town Hall was the center of community life at Randhurst. The facility dwarfed that of even Mount Prospect's village hall. It contained seating for four hundred people, a projection booth and a curtained stage, as well as access to food service. The company specifically noted that "these facilities are at the disposal of local civic and community groups for meetings and special events" and offered use of the facility free of charge to community groups. And used it was. In October 1962 alone, the facility was utilized by the Mount Prospect Junior Chamber of Commerce, the Children's Benefit League, the Little City Foundation, the Mount Prospect Rotary, the Lyric Opera, the Craig Manor Association, the Prospect Heights Improvement Association and the Council of Exceptional Children.

The state-of-the-art, four-hundred-seat auditorium known as the Randhurst Town Hall was used frequently by the company and the community.

The three massive department stores, Wieboldt's, Carson's and The Fair, flanked the Galleria like medieval fortifications. While the three anchor department stores had entered a cooperative effort to construct Randhurst, there would no doubt be some friendly competition. Like the center itself, the department stores would be an exercise in opulence. As an amazing example of how far these stores would go to attract shoppers and give the impression of luxury, one of the "superstars" of the center was the women's restroom at Wieboldt's. Shortly before Randhurst's grand opening, the *Herald* described the unveiling of the facility at a preview benefit:

> *"It's the most magnificent women's restroom this side of heaven," said a jubilant viewer of Wieboldt's women's lounge in Randhurst. During a preview benefit dinner dance Saturday night at Randhurst for the Mount Prospect Center of the Infant Welfare Society, women guests were given an opportunity to peek at the ornate powder room. It has been a conversation piece ever since details first leaked out about "what's to come at Randhurst." Now that it is finished and a few privileged ladies were given an opportunity to inspect it, the whole story can be told. It's bound to continue to be a conversation piece forever. Why? Because there are not enough superlatives to describe it. Everyone, men and women as well, (on opening day, that is) will inspect the room which actually defies description other than through a personal eye-view. The walls of the powder room, or entrance to the lounge, feature gold velvet panels on two sides and ebony glass on the others. The ceiling is a massive mosaic fashioned of hand-made Italian ceramic tiles and each tile handset. The colors feature reds, golds, burnt oranges, and a myriad of colors, all skillfully and artistically placed as to form a breath-taking brilliant motif. The floors are covered with handmade, handset gold Italian tiles. In the center of the lounge room is a large victorian red velvet circular lounge. Red velvet poufs are in front of each makeup mirror. The mirrors are framed with lights. In the center of the powder room over the circular lounge is a large crystal chandelier made to a special design in Italy. In the inner room where wash facilities are provided the floor is also tiled in gold. Three walls and the ceiling feature the same Italian mosaics as the ceiling in the powder room. The fourth wall is paneled in mirror from floor to ceiling. The lavatory bowls are set in slabs of deep red marble. Faucets are gold-plated. The doors of the "commodes" are of solid rosewood with inlaid gold medallions. Even the mop closet, outside the lounge, had to be in keeping with the ornate victorian motif. The doors of the cupboard are solid walnut, real French antiques over two centuries old. Nothing was spared*

to design the facility, which will be remembered, and visited, not always of necessity, but many times just to see if it's really true.

In addition to these luxurious "facilities," it appeared that Wieboldt's was specially targeting women at its Randhurst store. Wieboldt's went as far as to construct an out-lot automobile center that would cater to the "needs of women." It was described as

an ultra-modern automotive center pegged to the needs of woman shoppers at the Randhurst Shopping Center. The auto center, which is set apart from Wieboldt's department store there, offers such extras as an air-conditioned waiting room and pastel-colored showrooms and rest rooms. The center occupies 6,500 square feet of floor space, of which 3,000 square feet is devoted to eight car-service bays.

Wieboldt's, in addition to its desire to cater to the "needs of women," also catered heavily to children in the days of the grand opening. The store held a promotion entitled "Hands of the Future." On Friday, August 3, 250 local children imprinted their hands into the concrete floor of the east lobby. Children were presented with candy, soft drinks and savings bonds from the newly formed Randhurst Bank. Mount Prospect firefighters were on hand with a special "hand-washing station" pumped from a fire truck. Additionally, many of these youngsters were thrilled to learn that their handprints were accompanied by the paw prints of the beloved Mount Prospect fire mascot, Smokey the Dalmatian.[71]

Wieboldt's also proudly displayed a large six-foot-high mural produced by art students at seven art classes at Lincoln Junior High. The company retained the mural at its State Street store before it was placed in the supermarket area at the Randhurst store.[72]

Lincoln students were additionally honored by a reception of their art projects, featuring architectural models of homes hand-built by students, in the tenth-floor auditorium of Wieboldt's downtown location. The models were critiqued by four leading commercial architects of the day: Richard Brancik and Richard Conte, designers of Harlem-Irving Plaza; Raymond Brinker of Victor Gruen Associates; and Charles Martini, designer of Ford City, a new center that was being constructed on Chicago's South Side. An impressed Martini told reporters, "Some of these ideas are new and different. These youngsters have given me something to think about." The reception concluded with a "Coke-tail" party hosted by the students.[73]

Wieboldt's had colorful promotions throughout the early days at Randhurst, as this photo of an undated promotion for its supermarket implies.

As if this were not enough, Wieboldt's topped it all off by treating the children to a visit from Little Oscar and the infamous "Weinermobile" at the grand opening.

Speaking of children, another beloved feature of Randhurst was its public art. The building, at Gruen's insistence, contained hundreds of thousands of dollars' worth of art, especially sculpture. Much of it, which depicted animal forms, was favored by Randhurst's younger visitors. Generations of children fondly remember climbing and playing on these sculptures—so much so that George O'Neill stated he had received over fifty letters of complaint wondering why children were not prohibited from playing on the sculptured animals just a month after the grand opening. "The answer is simple," he laughed. "We put them there for the children to use." He did confess that "the children are rougher and stronger than anticipated, and several of the smaller animals have been torn loose from their moorings and have had to be re-anchored." He concluded by offering, "The horse weighs about 7,000 pounds, and I don't think they can do much with that, but I guess we'll just wait and see."[74]

The corporation announced in a special advertising section marking the grand opening of Randhurst:

It is difficult to find photos of Randhurst's public art without it being utilized by playing children. The "immovable" piece in this photo is Julie MacDonald's *Horses*.

> *Those who appreciate the arts will find a wealth of enjoyable things to view at Randhurst. Under the direction of Randhurst's architect Victor Gruen, some of the most famous sculptors in America were commissioned to create special works of art for a permanent display of sculpture at Randhurst's malls and Galleria.*[75]

The massive dome capping the Galleria was flanked by sculptures consisting of seventy-eight separate figures in precast concrete just under its interior, executed by Vern H. Walt of Los Angeles. The figures contained multicolored glass that gave the Galleria an awe-inspiring stained-glass effect when light coming through the base of the dome passed through them. Other sculptures included a three-branched form in wood set into concrete, created for the galleria by Jan de Swart, also of Los Angeles. Another Californian, Greg LaChapell, crafted a large elliptical disc, also located in the Galleria. Harold L. Kerr from nearby Palatine created a bronze sculpture called *Migration* depicting birds in flight. The beloved life-sized animals seen in the mall were the work of Pasadena artist Julie MacDonald and were carved from Portland limestone. A work in bronze by Arthur Mayfield Craft of Kansas City, Missouri, could be seen in the

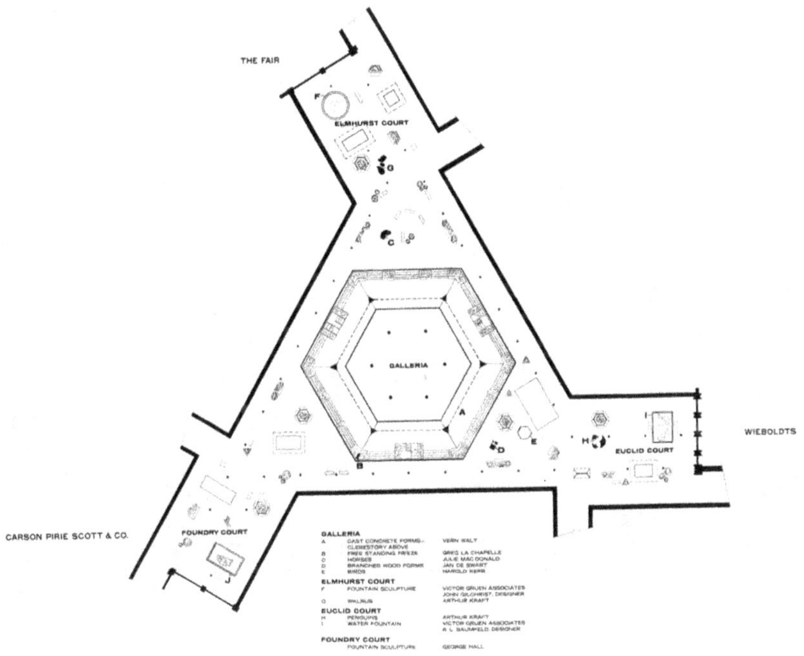

This diagram shows the locations, titles and artists behind the original, and numerous, sculptures at Randhurst.

center, as well as special water fountains by John Gilcrest and George W. Hall of Corona Del Mar, California.[76] While the fate of all the sculptures is unknown, following various redevelopments of Randhurst, some of the sculptures found new homes. MacDonald's *Horses*, seen in the photo on page 86, is now located in the courtyard of nearby Wheeling High School.

In the days leading up to the grand opening, Randhurst took the opportunity to introduce itself to its neighbors in Mount Prospect. In a community where a portion of the citizens had opposed its construction, the company was eager to show village residents that Randhurst would be beneficial and even a source of pride.

What's more, the presence of Randhurst reflected well on Mount Prospect. In various corporate publications and media reports, Mount Prospect was portrayed as one of Chicago's finest up-and-coming communities. Extensive research had been undertaken by real estate consulting firm and longtime Gruen shopping center collaborator Larry Smith & Company. A Randhurst Corporation prospectus proudly stated that Larry Smith & Company had concluded:

Sunlight pours past stained-glass sculptures and through the clerestory windows surrounding the dome—just one of many dramatic lighting effects originally used by Randhurst.

> *Mount Prospect was selected as the location for Randhurst Center after detailed study of surveys and reports on accessibility, economic stability and buying power of the surrounding communities. The results showed an active buying market...a trade area not affected by any other regional shopping center...an existing road system which is more than adequate for the expected traffic to and from Randhurst.*

Perhaps most importantly, the report found that

> *the Randhurst Trade Area has superior buying power! Young, growing families...with 25% above the average in Chicago. Per-family incomes have increased at a considerably higher rate than the national figure...And all indications point to a continuation of this trend.*[77]

The opening days of Randhurst were marked by promotions, spectacle and an influx of visitors the likes of which had never been seen in the area. The company reported that, remarkably, by its twenty-eighth day of operations, the center had received its one-millionth visitor. In true Randhurst fashion, the event was marked by a media blitz. The media declared that after a few short weeks, the winner of the Randhurst Jackpot was Joan Durham of nearby Audrey Lane.

She described herself to newspapers as "the one who never even gets anything out of a gumball machine." This quickly changed, as in addition to receiving a gift of one hundred dollars from Randhurst Bank (to, of course, be spent at Randhurst), Mrs. Durham was given the services of a governess for her six children and two maids to tidy her home, while a hired chauffeur and car took her and three friends to a complimentary lunch. Her day ended with a family dinner, also courtesy of the Randhurst Corporation. She remarked, "It was just wonderful… I'll never forget it. I'd like to come back again as the two-millionth shopper." She concluded that her lucky day was "a dream experience that left her numb."[78]

George M. O'Neill greets Randhurst's millionth shopper, Joan Durham, only twenty-eight days after the center opened.

While the daytime festivities were certainly spectacular, Randhurst also proved to be a stunning sight in the evening. The intrusion of lighting was a concern among residents of the formerly rural Mount Prospect. In a meet and greet with the nearby Prospect Heights Improvement Association, O'Neill addressed the worries about Randhurst and the vast amount of electricity required to illuminate it. He stated:

> *All building lighting has been designed as a part of the structures. There will be no neon store identifications to glare over the countryside. The lighting will be built into the outer walls of the three department stores, each with its own decorative and identifying pattern. Indirect lighting will be a feature of the outer walls of the other stores. It is expected that the total effect will be one of beauty, enhancing the area.*[79]

Gruen, always thinking in theatrical fashion, knew that lighting was an important feature to the attractiveness of any of his centers. From his earliest days designing Fifth Avenue storefronts, lighting played a key role in luring the shopper. So the evening of the grand-opening festivities was capped off by the use of Hollywood-style floodlights, which shone brightly into the suburban skies. The company promised shoppers that "specially designed lighting creates a breathtaking sight and adds a new thrill to evening shopping."[80]

Evenings at Randhurst also raised another, more serious, concern: security. The company's description of its ultramodern "electronic-age" alarm system alone was likely enough of a deterrent to ward off any would-be robbers:

> *The old town crier would be mighty proud to see his electronic age descendant in the new Randhurst. Centuries back when folks wanted to be assured of their security they relied on the wail of the crier—"Ten o'clock and all is well." Today, deep in the heart of Randhurst is a giant control board. Its indicator lights flash at a hundred positions. Instantaneously it sets off an electronic typewriter that banks out a message. This is the Randhurst "watchman."*

This dramatic promotional photo of The Fair during the grand opening showcases the center's "light architecture."

Every door in Randhurst is wired to the central electronic watchman. Each has a code number and its own light station on the giant control board. If the last man to leave Carson's, for example, forgets to lock one of the doors at the Carson entrance, the electronic watchman will light up. The typewriter will indicate the code number of the door that is open. The door can be locked quickly when its location is noted. Checking all the locks just once a day for Randhurst—world's largest shopping center under one roof—would be more than a fulltime job for any one human watchman. But it is accomplished continuously by the electronic watchman. The special Randhurst system was installed and designed expressly for the center by Notifier Electric Co. of Chicago.

Early shoppers recall that the interior lighting in the center was also quite dramatic. The dim, recessed lighting caused the storefronts to pop, even during daylight. The overall effect, much like a church, was one of hushed awe. This effect can be seen in early photographs of the center. One of

The subdued interior lighting gave the overall effect of walking down a street at dusk, enhancing the center's "outdoor effect." One of the best examples of this, as well as one of the most aesthetically striking stores in the center, was the Singer Sewing Machine Store, designed by Frank Lloyd Wright apprentice Don Erickson. *Image courtesy of the children of Don Erickson—Karyn, Don and Elizabeth Erickson and Shay Dam-Erickson. Used with permission.*

the stores that best exemplified this effect was the Singer Sewing Machine Store, adjacent to The Fair. The store was designed by northwest suburban architect Don Erickson. In a twist of fate, Frank Lloyd Wright, for as much as he criticized Gruen's Southdale Center, would have something of a legacy at Randhurst through Erickson's store design. Erickson served as an apprentice to Wright at the legendary Taliesin Fellowship in Wisconsin from 1948 to 1951. As the story goes, while Erickson was attending the University of Illinois, he told one of his architecture professors, "Frank Lloyd Wright would do it this way," to which the professor replied, "If you like him so much, go to him." While on a smaller scale, the design of the store bears a striking resemblance to the "lily pads" of Wright's "great workroom" at the S.E. Johnson Wax Building in Kenosha, Wisconsin.[81]

Another interesting part of Randhurst was out of public view. This feature was very much a product of its time. Cold War tensions between the Americans and the Soviets were peaking in the otherwise festive days of Randhurst's grand opening. They would come to a head in the Cuban Missile Crisis, which was a few short weeks away. As a result, Randhurst boasted a fallout shelter in its massive underground. The shelter, complete with bunks and showers, was said to be able to hold every resident of Mount Prospect in the instance of nuclear strike on Chicago. It was further rumored that the shelter was constructed in order to discourage residents from constructing individual shelters, which were seen as unsightly and many of which were, for lack of a better term, "homemade." The Village of Mount Prospect had reluctantly agreed to allow shelters to be built under stringent conditions shortly before Randhurst's construction. A 1961 newspaper report discussed the issue, noting that James E. Wax, chairman of the architectural committee, had informed Mayor Schlaver that while village code did not provide specifically for such shelters, several inquiries and one permit application for construction of a family fallout shelter had been received. The application requested that the location of such shelter be permitted in the thirty-foot front setback area. Wax stated that this was not allowable under the present zoning ordinance. Clearly, this issue was a hot topic in the community and a complicated one for village authorities, as seen in an article in the *Mount Prospect Herald* on August 10, 1961. Whether Randhurst would have been a suitable fallout shelter was fortunately never put to the test, but this was most likely a way for the village government to put this complex, and annoying, issue to rest once and for all.

The underground labyrinth of Randhurst also served a more utilitarian purpose: truck deliveries and the massive job of keeping Randhurst supplied. The company, ever alluding to the theater, noted:

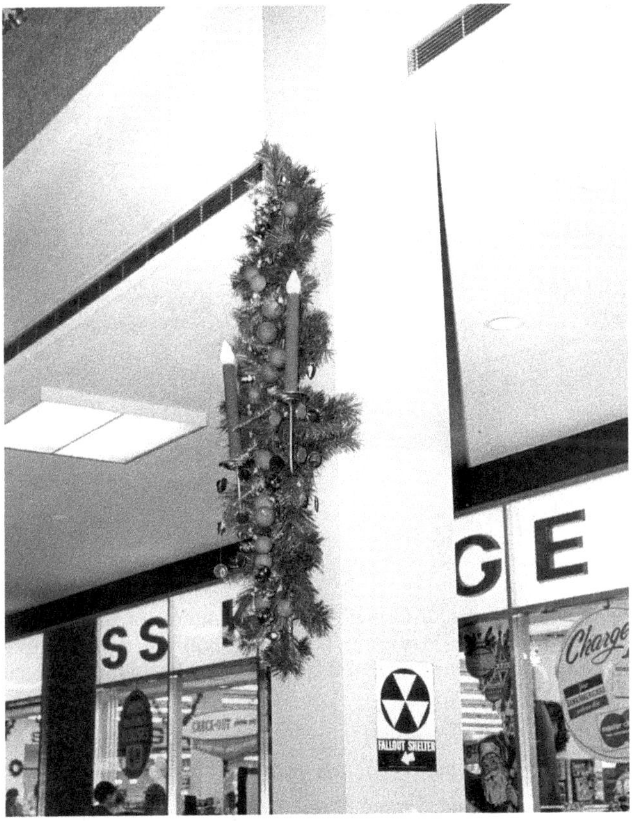

Randhurst opened weeks before the Cuban Missile Crisis. Its fallout shelter, located in the basement level, was said to be able to accommodate every resident of Mount Prospect.

Every production has its backstage crew...Backstage at Randhurst is all underground. A service tunnel providing 10,000 square feet of loading dock winds it way beneath the 1,200,000 square feet above. Allowing over 100 trucks at any time to deliver their wares and pick up merchandise, food, and equipment needed in the giant center's operations. A labyrinth of pipes and ducts are suspended from the ceilings of the tunnel. Through the maze of lines, heat, light, power and air conditioning are conveyed to stores above. The service tunnel is wide enough to allow a free flow of traffic. It follows a triangular path around the underground core of the center. Special access driveways to the tunnel are provided for the trucks to eliminate their traveling the driveways and parking lot areas reserved for customers. Safety and convenience were the primary motives for separating the shipping and receiving traffic from the pedestrian and automobile traffic. In addition, the noise and exhaust from the trucks will not be noticed by the shoppers. The service tunnel is the main activity of operation for Randhurst. It has

Among the criteria for Gruen's shopping centers was that all truck traffic and merchandise deliveries were to be made completely separate from and out of sight of pedestrian areas—underground in the case of Randhurst, as seen in this photo.

> *been used during the construction stage to bring building materials into the triangular center. In the past few weeks, merchants' trucks have used the tunnel to stock the three full line department stores and many other specialty and service shops and professional offices. Traffic control in the tunnel is accomplished by a modern automatic system of warning lights. The vehicles all move one-way thru the tunnel.*[82]

Randhurst officials also sought to invoke the sublimity of nature. They took the "outdoor effect" of the center quite seriously, devoting a large amount of expertise and money to the endeavor. Especially during the brutal Chicago winter months, the center's tropical décor would go a long way to entice customers to "vacation" at Randhurst. The *Mount Prospect Herald* reported that the center would borrow "a little bit of Florida," literally, to decorate the center. Franz Lipp served as the center's landscape architect. Much like Victor Gruen, Lipp was a disciple of Frederick Law Olmsted. In the spirit of Olmsted's planning of Riverside, Lipp worked diligently to ensure that plantings were meticulously selected but placed in a manner that would make them look random, as if placed by Mother Nature. The foliage included palm trees twenty feet high, rubber plants ten to fifteen feet tall and other tropical greenery that grew in seven large octagonal tree pits around the galleria. The pits were twelve feet in diameter and eight feet deep. Blooming flowers were intermingled with the greenery and tropical plants in large tile-walled planters, which lined the upper level and draped over the walls. Other large planters and flower boxes, many of which were appropriately triangular, were filled with blossoms of the particular season (chrysanthemums and roses in summer, poinsettias in winter and tulips in the spring), with greenery of various kinds placed along the iron railings at the stairways and fences that surrounded the open restaurant in the Pavilion in the center of the Galleria.

The *Herald* assured visitors to Randhurst:

> *The atmosphere of the flowers, trees and plants…will be one of beauty and relaxation—cool in the summer and warm in the winter. The flowers, trees and plants will blend with fountains, sculptures and other works of art, bringing an outdoor garden atmosphere indoors.*

The paper also described the lengths to which landscape architect Franz Lipp went to ensure that the proper plantings were obtained for Randhurst. The *Herald* informed its readers:

> *Actually, while the finished setting will appear effortless, as nature would intend such a garden to look—there is a story in back of the planting project which sounds like a miracle about to come true—as a result of long hours of planning, hard work and much tender loving care. For the trees didn't actually grow from a seedling dropped in the center by a songbird of the south. They were dreamed of by Franz Lipp, landscape architect for Randhurst. Lipp designed the plant settings and decided what should go in each to make the world's largest shopping center a work of art.*

Lipp and his wife went to Florida in April 1962 and personally selected each tree and plant. They purchased only the most perfect and supervised the pruning while there. The plants were not bought from any one grower but from a number of growers in several places in the general area of Miami. The Lipps supervised the first pruning to see that the roots would not be injured or shocked. They also saw to it that the plants and trees were properly "hardened" through a special two-month acclimation treatment, necessary to ensure safe shipment north. The trees were balled and burlapped and planted in large boxes for shipment in two huge refrigerator trucks to Gus Grundstrom's Greenhouse in Glenview.

As a testament to just how important the plantings were to the center, Grundstrom had to build shelters, especially for the large trees. In these structures, the trees were carefully replanted and protected and were given additional acclimation treatment until they were moved into their new permanent home in the arcades of Randhurst on August 1. Lipp was assisted in the project by Homer Lang, a "well known florist in the area," and Carl Pathe, a Mount Prospect resident and landscape engineer with Lipp's firm. In the days leading up to the grand opening, the newspaper reported that

> *the job the horticulturalists have at the present time is to see that the plantings do not get a shock. They must be kept in a place where the humidity is conducive to tropical plants, but in a much lower temperature than Florida. They must be trained to survive in a lower, more comfortable temperature designed especially for area shoppers—not trees.*

The *Herald* concluded that "the landscape architects say they are not endeavoring to create a tropical atmosphere necessarily, but to provide a pleasant, fresh setting in keeping with the motif of the Center."[83]

All of these important physical aspects of Randhurst were in conjunction with Victor Gruen's principles. He took the opportunity to dote heavily

The palm trees, "a little bit of Florida," were lifted into place, flanking the Galleria, days before the opening of the center.

on the many meticulous features of the center in the days after the grand opening, telling a Chicago construction publication, "Randhurst was planned not only to serve the shopping needs of the surrounding population, but by virtue of its environmental characteristics, to become a social meeting ground and civic and cultural point."

He continued:

> *The concept of complete separation of pedestrians, autos and trucks, which has proven so successful in our other center designs, was an important guide in the design of Randhurst. Randhurst is a completed expression of the "introverted" center. All stores face the interior, enclosed, air conditioned pedestrian spaces. No stores, with the exception of the major department stores, are entered directly from the parking areas, nor do they display signs or identification of any kind at the exterior. Thereby, the elimination of the natural tendency for retailers to compete for visual attention provides an overall exterior design integrity. Thus, Randhurst Center appears to*

Randhurst architect Victor Gruen, a prolific author and speaker on the subject of shopping centers, described Randhurst as "different from any other established building type."

the viewers from the surrounding highways and the parking areas as an architectural expression distinctly different from that usually associated with shopping centers, but also different from any other established building type. Though the individualities of the three department stores are expressed, there is harmony established between them, tying them together with the uniformly developed design of the exterior of the store wings between them. Liveliness and attractiveness have been achieved by a sculptured and highly textured treatment and by color differentiation which in daytime are brought out by sunlight and shadow and which through the introduction of "light architecture" are dramatized by the employment of concealed light.[84]

Even when it was closed, Randhurst continued to draw crowds. The *Chicago Tribune* reported that on the Sunday following the center's grand opening, thousands of cars trekked to Mount Prospect to get a look at the massive center, despite the fact that it was closed on Sundays. Mount Prospect police officers were dispatched to the center to control traffic on the swollen thoroughfares and to regulate the crowds. The newspaper reported

Patrons jam the stairwells in the days of Randhurst's grand opening.

The parking lot at Randhurst, looking south toward the water tower, approached capacity during the days of its grand opening in 1962. Note the large spotlight in the foreground.

that "about 2,300 persons jammed the grounds of the mammoth center and surrounding highways as they spent a Sunday afternoon window shopping."

Now that Randhurst had opened amidst great fanfare, capturing the attention of the Chicago area, it was ready to face the 1960s. This was a tumultuous period for America, and Randhurst would act as a product of its time, taking the cultural changes in stride. Randhurst officials realized early on that it would not remain the sole regional shopping center in the northwest suburbs for long and sought to continue the new shopping center's tradition of convention-defying promotions.

As one newspaper concluded following the grand opening:

> *Randhurst's presence here can be seen as one of mutual benefit. Its recognition of the northwest suburban area as a retail shopping outlet is obvious. Its contributions to the northwest suburbs should also be apparent. We welcome them to this bustling, booming area, and wish them every success.*[85]

6

"This Well-Rounded, Hitch-Proof Program"

The Randhurst Plan of the 1960s

Frustrative Last-Year-Itis

Around the turn of a new year many of us—and particularly those of us in the retail business—become highly susceptible to a special type of disease known as "last-year-itis." It's contagious unfortunately and is characterized by the compulsive use of last year's methods, systems, schedules, advertising and promotions…

We are living in a changing time. It's been said that half of the merchandise now on sale in today's stores was not even on the market 5 to 10 years ago.

Markets change—people's buying power changes too. It is essential to be competitive and to give your market what they need & want. New approaches are called for if new customers are to be attracted to your store.

Keep abreast of what's new in your field, in your Center, in your market. Try to adapt this innovation to your particular solution. This will enable you to look forward to a successful sales period. Don't let "Last-year-itis" hinder your merchandising and your promotions.

Harold J. Carlson
Randhurst Vice-President and General Manager
January 6, 1966

Suburban Chicago's Grandest Shopping Center

After its whirlwind grand opening, Randhurst was determined to keep shoppers coming well after the confetti was swept up. In what would come to define the center, as well as mall promotions in general, the 1960s saw an onslaught of various promotions that would keep Randhurst as Chicagoland's foremost shopping center, as well as make it a focal point for community organizations. Randhurst, and its supporting Merchants Association, was serious about these promotions and dedicated a serious amount of revenue to it. In 1963 alone, the Randhurst Merchants Association spent a whopping $32,000 (nearly $250,000 in 2010) on promotions. In accordance with the corporation's wishes to make shopping an "event," there was always an excuse to go to Randhurst.

Two weeks after its grand opening, Randhurst hosted what would seem to be a rather unusual event for a posh, modern shopping center but spoke to the makeup of the area at the time: the sixteenth annual North Cook County 4-H Fair. The three-day event was held from August 23 to 25. The event included "hundreds of special exhibits prepared by 4-H youngsters…a 4-H talent show, and the crowning of the 1962 4-H King and Queen." The event even hosted "75 head of livestock."[86] The *Mount Prospect Herald* happily announced that the event would have an exciting culmination in that "the old national barn dance with WGN will be broadcasting a Saturday night show Aug. 25 direct from Randhurst."[87] With palpable excitement, the newspaper went on to declare:

> *Final arrangements for this appearance have now been made and Bob Atcher will be appearing on the show. Bob Atcher is a daily host to many radio listeners in our northwest suburban area as well as appearing regularly on the WGN* Barn Dance *shows. Atcher is Kentucky-born and has sung his way into the hearts of millions, with his special way of doing the old-time "story songs." He is an excellent horseman* [and] *an expert marksman… Long a favorite of radio and television audiences, he is a recording star for Capitol* [Records] *in the country and western fields.*[88]

Events would occur years later to suggest that Atcher was deeply impressed by what he saw at Randhurst.

Another early publicity event was an automobile show. This was appropriately, but perhaps unintentionally, a nod to the power of the automobile, which made the creation of a massive center like Randhurst possible in the first place. It was also put on much to the chagrin of the organizers of Chicago's Annual Auto Show. While the residents of

Mike Brittle of the Palatine 4-H Club exhibits his champion sheep at Randhurst's first major event, the North Cook County 4-H Fair, attended by an estimated 250,000.

Mount Prospect slept, sixty 1963 models representing all the American manufacturers were wheeled into Randhurst. This occurrence interestingly revealed that the glass arcade entrances could be opened in their entirety to allow automobiles to be driven in and placed throughout the center—such exhibitions had been given great consideration in Randhurst's design. Even though the car show was held in October (three full months before the Chicago Auto Show, which was even at that time recognized as the biggest in the country), the *Tribune* noted that "the Chicago Automobile Trade association frowns on the enterprise." Ed Clearly, the executive secretary, scornfully declared:

> *We have advised our membership that they might waste money and efforts in so-called auto shows that use the new models as an attraction to other merchandise. In contrast, the association's annual show is concentrated solely on promotion of automobile sales.*

A defiant Randhurst spokesman proudly bragged that these new automobiles would be parked "amid the landscaping and sculpture of the world's largest enclosed shopping center." The paper additionally mentioned that, despite the opposition by the trade association, the Northern Cook County dealers endorsed the event.[89]

An additional large, recurring event was the Randhurst Art Fair. The fair attracted artists from all over the Chicagoland area. It was a logical event for the center, given its large financial commitment to public art, which had defined the center's construction under Victor Gruen Associates. Paintings,

Randhurst's arcade entrances were opened in the evening to wheel in 1963 automobiles for an exposition in late 1962. This clever modification allowed many large events at Randhurst.

sculptures and photographs graced every corner of the center, giving these "starving artists" a chance to display and sell their work. Prizes were awarded by the Randhurst Corporation in various categories.

While for the most part things were going quite smoothly in the weeks following the grand opening, there were some complaints. At a meeting of the Prospect Heights Improvement Association, O'Neill addressed a "medium-sized audience," whose chief concern was the "clutter and inconvenience" of a popcorn stand, which also sold soft drinks and sandwiches. O'Neill admitted that the concession stand seemed out of context with its immediate surroundings in the "newest and most luxurious shopping attraction." Ever the salesman, however, O'Neill added, "But, speaking from the standpoint of a practical business venture, we have concluded that we can afford to clean up a lot of popcorn and litter for the profit we expect to realize from this little 400 square foot hunk of floor space." The paper concluded, "Don't feel sorry for that popcorn vendor the next time you see him! He has a good thing going, especially if he operates a concession at Randhurst Shopping Center."[90]

Also in the weeks following the grand opening, change immediately began to hit Randhurst. An internal company publication announced:

> *It is with great regret that we announce the resignation of George M. O'Neill, Vice-President and General Manager of the Randhurst Corporation. Mr. O'Neill's resignation becomes effective sometime during the latter part of January. We wish to echo here the many good wishes and expressions for success Mr. O'Neill has received regarding his new venture.*

A panoramic view of Randhurst's interior, circa 1962, shows the offending popcorn stand in the foreground.

O'Neill, who had served as the capable face of Randhurst throughout its development and construction, announced that his "new venture" was to accept a position as the executive vice-president and director of the Chicago Industrial District, Inc. The company was developing another massive shopping center on the city's southwest side, Ford City. Ford City borrowed its name from a defunct World War II–era jet-engine plant that was later operated by the Ford Motor Company and would be converted into, a scant seven months after Randhurst opened, what was billed as the largest shopping center in the world. The center would boast thirty acres of stores under one roof. This would certainly not be the last time Randhurst would be outdone.[91]

Another major change came quickly to Randhurst when it was announced that The Fair would cease operations. As it was the last store to bear the company's name, it would be the first to be transitioned and was given the Montgomery Ward nameplate in November 1963 after just a year of operation. Montgomery Ward would remain a stable anchor store at Randhurst for an additional three decades.

Despite these changes, less than a year after its opening, the *Chicago Tribune* noted that Randhurst was having its desired effect and announced that services had jumped in Mount Prospect, citing Randhurst as the main reason. Assistant to the village manager David Yost reported in early July 1963 that retail sales tax receipts, primarily from Randhurst, were being used to increase services and reduce taxes in the community. He told the *Tribune* that the village was now able to offer free garbage pickup and purchase a backhoe tractor for digging holes and trenches, as well as two dump trucks. The water system capacity was

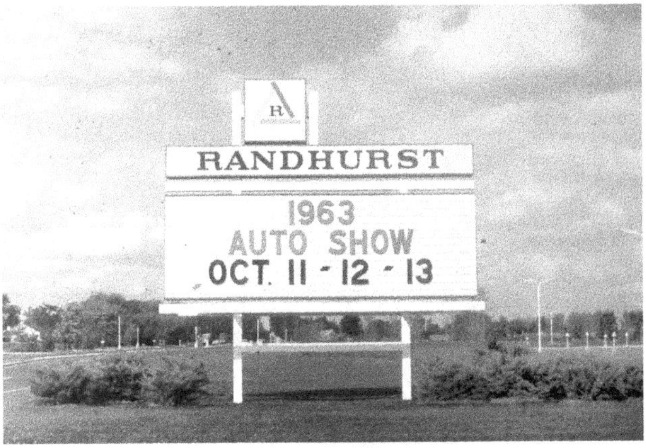

Randhurst's handsome marquee announced the center's unique and varied events throughout the 1960s, in this case the first auto show.

also increased by the addition of more wells. These new tax revenues covered the $25,000 annual cost of the village's Dutch elm program, which included the pruning, spraying and removal of dead elm trees. Additionally, the village hired five new firemen and five new police officers at salaries of $6,000 and a village engineer and draftsman for the engineering department. Mount Prospect finance director James King noted that the tax rate had been slashed by 7 percent and told the newspaper that village tax revenues in the past year had nearly doubled, skyrocketing from $117,000 to $231,000. A confident King stated, "We're doing everything possible we can and we're adding a lot of everything." Yost echoed these sentiments: "Any monies enhance services by the village, including police and fire protection, maintenance, and all other areas."[92] Mount Prospect and the surrounding area's charity groups and community organizations continued to, in turn, utilize the center immeasurably. Police, fire and state and local government expositions, exhibits and programs, in addition to commercial ventures such as countless automobile, boat, home and garden shows, were regular occurrences throughout the years.

Some of the most meaningful memories of Randhurst, especially among children, came from Christmastime. Randhurst pulled out all the stops to attract shoppers to the center during the busy holiday season. The first Christmas at Randhurst saw the center decorated extravagantly, with what was billed as the "world's largest chandelier" suspended above the massive dome. Other years saw the extravagance continue with such items as a two-and-a-half-story, sixteen-foot-wide Christmas tree. While commercialization of Christmas is largely viewed as a relatively recent phenomenon, the internal *Randhurst Reporter* of January 10, 1963, proves otherwise. Promotion Director Charles MacKenzie concluded gleefully:

Promotions such as the "Randhurst Hootenanny" drew thousands of people. Countless publicity stunts like this were held at the center throughout the years.

Christmas was a memorable time for many of the first Randhurst shoppers. This massive decoration suspended from the dome was known as the "world's largest chandelier."

The Randhurst Christmas Program was a "Titanic" success, phrasing it mildly—big and powerful. All of us at Randhurst can take collective pride in having been a part of this well-rounded, hitch-proof program. From Santa's rocket arrival to the last click of the key that locked the center on Christmas Eve, an air of success, satisfaction and pride prevailed. Everyone associated with Randhurst retained the holiday spirit throughout the entire six week period. The stores and sales personnel remained slim and attractive. Randhurst in all of its Christmas splendor was enchanting and each day was made more pleasant for the holiday shopper. It is now up to all of us to maintain this high standard through the year. December sales figures indicate that people find what they want at Randhurst. This trend indicates that 1963 will be a successful and prosperous one for all at Randhurst.[93]

Another popular, and certainly unique, Christmastime feature involved Randhurst's water tower. With the assistance of a crane, the tower was festooned with lights that were attached to a basket just below its tank. This gave the tower the effect of an illuminated hot-air balloon. Generations of Mount Prospect children recall Santa waving to them from the basket, high above the intersections of Rand, Elmhurst and Foundry Roads, enticing families to visit the center.

During the Christmas season, Randhurst's water tower ornately doubled as "Santa's Hot-Air Balloon." The decorations were put in place by a large crane.

The first Christmas at Randhurst was also the first try at a marketing promotion that would come to define shopping centers across the nation: the celebrity appearance. While certainly Randhurst was not the first to concoct the notion that celebrities would attract patrons, it was a staple of Randhurst's marketing program, and countless Chicago and national luminaries would visit Randhurst over the years. The first was Cuban-American Cesar Romero, who appeared in late November 1962 to welcome Santa Claus on his aforementioned, and appropriately space-aged, "rocket arrival," as well as to sign autographs. While today

Among the first of many celebrity visitors to Randhurst was Cuban-American actor Cesar Romero, famous for his role as the Joker on the *Batman* television series.

he is known for his legendary portrayal of the Joker on the 1960s television series *Batman*, by 1962 he had countless film and television appearances under his belt, including the original incarnation of *Ocean's Eleven* starring Frank Sinatra and his "Rat Pack" in 1960. Romero was also credited with bringing the character of the "Latin Lover" into the American lexicon through his various film roles. Interestingly, when he appeared at Randhurst, his famous role as the Joker was still four years away. It is likely that the company hired Romero hoping that his Cuban ancestry would evoke thoughts of the island itself in what could have been a cross-promotion to prop up the tropical theme of the first Christmas, underscoring the center's indoor comfort. Cuba in the early 1960s was also very much under the microscope during the missile standoff with the Soviet Union.

In the later years of the 1960s and '70s, Randhurst began a tradition of having Norbert Locke, better known to generations of Chicago youth as "Ringmaster Ned," from the beloved WGN children's show *Bozo's Circus*, kickoff the Christmas season on the weekend following Thanksgiving. As if his appearance were not dramatic enough for scores of children, Locke arrived by helicopter. He was often accompanied by Cooky the Clown.

Throughout Randhurst's history, celebrities, musicians, athletes and authors, known and unknown, drew shoppers to the center. Some of the

Norbert "Ringmaster Ned" Locke of the beloved *Bozo's Circus* television show, costume in hand, arrives by helicopter to welcome the Christmas shopping season at Randhurst.

Randhurst hosted countless local and national celebrities and popular "tough guys" throughout the years, including Lou Ferrigno, Mr. T and, pictured here, Arnold Schwarzenegger, presumably promoting a book on bodybuilding.

Throngs of people visited Randhurst in October 1966 to welcome Senator Robert F. "Bobby" Kennedy when he made his last visit to Chicago in order to campaign for fellow senator Paul Douglas.

better-known stars included a young basketball standout from the Chicago Bulls named Michael Jordan and "tough guys" Arnold Schwarzenegger, Lou Ferrigno and Mr. T, as well as Chicago Bears quarterback Gary Huff. It would appear that many of these celebrities served the dual purpose of giving northwest suburban husbands a reason to look forward to a trip to the center.

In addition to film and television stars, Randhurst also welcomed political superstars. The 1960s, especially in Chicago, would prove to be a tumultuous period, reaching a national boiling point at the 1968 Democratic National Convention. In the years leading up to this event, Randhurst was home to a historic meeting of politicians on October 16, 1966, when Chicago mayor Richard J. Daley and Illinois senator Paul H. Douglas welcomed a charming future presidential candidate named Robert F. Kennedy to a rally outside the center to support the midterm elections of 1966. Signs with slogans such as "'72 May Be Too Late, Kennedy in '68" and "All Chicago Welcomes Bob Kennedy" greeted him. The Chicago news corps, this time armed with television cameras, again gathered at Randhurst to cover the political rock star's visit. It was likely that Kennedy made this visit to incur favor from Mayor Daley, who was seen as a kingmaker in the Democratic Party and was widely credited, for better or worse, with securing the state of Illinois for John F. Kennedy in the controversial election of 1960. Sadly, Senator Kennedy would never again visit the city. Like his brother, he was felled by an assassin's bullet in the summer of 1968, just before he would have made his triumphant return to the Chicago convention to seek his party's

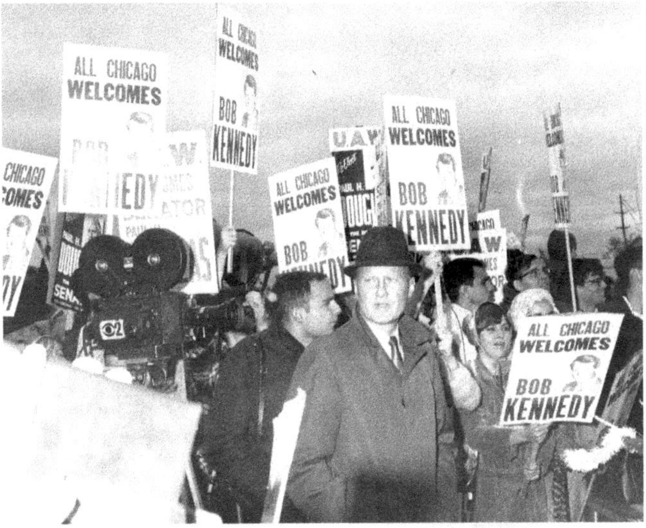

It was reported that the crowd, "captivated by the Kennedy mystique," stretched from just outside the center to the water tower.

nomination for president. Longtime Randhurst official Paul Dasso recalled that the crowd stretched from the stage, which was located under the water tower, all the way to the Montgomery Ward store. Dasso reported that the crowd contained both Republicans and Democrats, and he was proud that Randhurst offered residents an opportunity to be "captivated by the Kennedy mystique."[94] Richard Nixon, who would prove to be the victorious candidate in the election of 1968, visited nearby Prospect High School on October 21, 1968, less than three weeks before the election. Randhurst Center was used as the guiding landmark on posters directing well-wishers to the event.

The underground bomb shelter in Randhurst, as previously stated, was fortunately never put to the test. However, Randhurst was used as an emergency shelter in the 1960s. The notorious blizzard in February 1967 crippled Chicago and the surrounding areas, leaving hundreds of thousands of residents and travelers stranded, store shelves empty and thousands of schoolchildren thrilled. Dasso recalled that Randhurst was closed for four days, but approximately half of the staff stayed there. The center was also opened up to stranded customers and passersby. It appeared that it was a rather comfortable stay, as the center had virtually every creature comfort imaginable, and the center's restaurants were able to provide plentiful meals.

In addition to Dasso's memories of RFK's visit and the Blizzard of '67, the center was also home to some very personal experiences. He recalled that his memories of Randhurst began with a broom. He was just out of the army and was waiting for the State Department examination to become a

This exhibition in the 1960s showcased a fully functional "Futura" swimming pool. According to reports, it was constructed in just eighty-four man-hours and seen by over 350,000 people.

Foreign Service officer. He took what he thought was a temporary position at the construction office, where he swept floors. He rose through the ranks, eventually becoming the general administrator and marketing director and, later, manager of the center. As he told it, the more he got acquainted with Randhurst, the more he fell in love with it, quite literally as it turns out. In 1962, while applying for an automobile loan at the Randhurst Bank, he met a young installment loan officer named Sue, who took his application and interviewed him. While he did not say whether he received the loan, he certainly received more than he anticipated. Paul and Sue were married three years later in 1965. Sue was also quite active in the center, having a hand in establishing the Americana Shop and the Patisserie Bakery and later starting and operating the Bon Appétit restaurant.

The 1960s saw Randhurst become the triumph it was planned to be in the late 1950s. While the nation changed, so did Randhurst. Its various promotions and celebrity visitors reflected the times. Snow wasn't the only thing that piled up in Randhurst in 1967. The '60s were exponentially

Randhurst Bank, site of the fateful meeting between Paul and Sue Dasso.

successful years for Randhurst. The *Prospect Day* noted early in 1968 that Randhurst had reported record sales in 1967. Dasso told the *Day* that "Christmas shopping started in early November and leveled off towards the end of the month…The last two weeks before Christmas were fantastic." He also reported that January 1968 was a strong month in comparison to previous years and that sales for the 1967 fiscal year totaled $66 million, a 10.0 percent increase from 1966. The Village of Mount Prospect also enjoyed increased benefits from a sales tax increase from 4.5 to 5.0 percent on August 1, 1967. The village netted about $490,000, which accounted for approximately a quarter of its entire operating budget.[95]

However, with the dawn of the 1970s, Randhurst would face serious challenges as Mount Prospect and the surrounding suburbs began to grow beyond control. These communities would soon form new identities that would redefine the role of shopping centers. Moreover, Mount Prospect's neighbors looked with envy at Randhurst, since their residents—and more importantly, their expendable income—were flocking to the center. Whether it was ready for it or not, Randhurst Shopping Center would soon be locked into a serious case of sibling rivalry.

7

"From Satellite to Self-Containment"

Randhurst and the "Technoburbs" of the 1970s

Meet the "new America"

> *Northwest suburbia: A place where new-found self-containment may be perpetuated as the children of residents settle down in their home communities instead of answering the once-powerful call of the big city and its job market. A collection of suburbs which no longer depend on Chicago and whose remaining links with it grow a bit weaker each year… An intravenous hose in reverse, pumping economic juices out of the problem-punchy big city. No skyscrapers yet, but that may be next.*[96]

As Randhurst Shopping Center marked its first decade of existence, it was joined by many siblings. The birth of Randhurst's greatest sibling rival was announced in the last weeks of the 1960s. Ground was broken for Woodfield Mall in October 1969. The center would be situated at Golf Road and Illinois Highway 53 in Schaumburg, a scant five miles from Randhurst. The *Tribune* announced that the center would cost a colossal $90 million, occupy 191 acres and contain 160 stores. The center would be anchored by Sears, Roebuck & Co., Marshall Field & Company and the J.C. Penney Company.[97]

If imitation is the sincerest form of flattery, then Schaumburg's Woodfield Mall was an exercise in the flattery of Randhurst on an imposing scale. While Victor Gruen and the Randhurst Corporation may have begged to differ, Taubman & Homart, the developers of the massive center, touted that they were "making Woodfield a retail environment totally different from any other center in the Chicago area," and the mall would feature "three levels of walkways and courts, linked by carpeted ramps, stairs and escalators…accented with sculptures, two-level pools, special displays and an aquarium…More than 100 skylights—some more than 20 feet across—will give the shopping center an 'open atmosphere.'" Perhaps the greatest similarity to Randhurst was that Woodfield was billed as the largest enclosed retail center in the world.[98]

By May 1970, the *Tribune* reported that the foundation work had been completed and that the steel backbone of the center had been raised. Echoing Randhurst's unapologetic girth, Woodfield's three anchor stores alone would occupy over 300,000 square feet each, nearly the same square footage as the entirety of Randhurst. Sears and Marshall Field's would represent each retailer's largest stores in Chicagoland, while the J.C. Penney store would be the company's largest out of its almost seventeen hundred stores nationwide.[99]

The mayor of Schaumburg, who oversaw the construction and grand opening of Woodfield, was a one-time guest of honor at Randhurst—none other than Robert O. "Bob" Atcher, the famous country western singer and performer who had hosted a live broadcast of the WGN *Barn Dance* at the 4-H Fair two weeks after Randhurst's grand opening. He now prepared his own grand opening for the media.

However, because each anchor store, and the land they were built on, was owned by its respective company, Woodfield's grand opening proved to be somewhat anticlimactic. While it had swollen to 215 proposed retail outlets, the center's debut occurred as it stood half completed, with its anchor stores having opened over a month beforehand and only 60 retailers officially open for business. Mayor Atcher, along with actors Carol Lawrence and Vincent Price, snipped a large orange ribbon in front of a crowd estimated "optimistically" at a mere twenty-five thousand. Reporters Gerald West and Ronald Yates, noting the lack of refinement of the ceremonies, asked their readers:

> *What happens when you hold a grand opening at the world's largest shopping center when the place is only half finished? The answer is grimy construction workers gingerly sidestepping suburban mothers laden with packages and babies, seemingly miles of electrical cable strewn in and out of half-finished stores, and several hundred persons wandering about with lost looks on their faces.*

woodfield
World's largest
enclosed regional retail development.
Sears, J C Penney, Marshall Field & Company, Lord & Taylor.
More than 200 specialty shops and services,
including theaters, restaurants, ice arena.
Owners: Woodfield Associates
Management/Leasing Agents:
The Taubman Company, Inc./Southfield, Michigan
Golf Road at Route 53
Schaumburg, Ill.
54
Commerce

Woodfield Mall, located approximately five miles from Randhurst, opened in 1971 and would continually upstage Randhurst.

The reporters noted that Woodfield's manager, the aptly named Jerry O'Neil, took them on a tour of the nearly 2-million-square-foot center and showed off Woodfield's features "like a mother showing off her baby's newest tooth." O'Neil reassured them, "This has to be the world's largest center for a long time to come, for two reasons...First, we can expand to 2.1 million square feet anytime, and second, there are few places in the world with wall-to-wall people like we have in this northwest suburban area." O'Neil also pointed out, familiarly, that Woodfield would soon be used as a venue for an auto show and that the center had a large theater-like area for various performances and exhibitions.[100] As an interesting side note, actor Vincent Price offered much more than a celebrity photo-op. In addition to his grand-opening duties, Mr. Price, by special arrangement, conducted hourly talks in the carpeting department of Sears on the subjects of art, gourmet cooking and home decorating. Being quite the connoisseur, he brought with him a selection of paintings from the Vincent Price Gallery of Fine Arts, an exclusive brand of art available for sale in more upscale Sears stores.[101]

Also much like Randhurst, Woodfield was astronomically successful financially. In its first year of operations, the center generated well over its estimate of $160 million in sales, and the Village of Schaumburg was netting $120,000 per month in sales tax revenue, up from its previous monthly average of $50,000. A proud Mayor Atcher beamed, "We deliberately developed Schaumburg as a paycheck center for the northwest suburbs. Back in the days when no one even thought of locating industry here, the village designated one chunk of 4,000 acres for industry and commerce."[102] Undoubtedly, Atcher, by all accounts a very shrewd businessman, had taken notice of Randhurst's success when performing his *Barn Dance* duties there just after the grand opening of 1962. By the spring of 1972, the *Chicago Tribune* noted that Woodfield was hitting pay dirt and that the neighboring suburbs were feeling the bite, having mixed opinions about the gargantuan center.

Some were angry. An openly unhappy community was Schaumburg neighbor Hoffman Estates. Elmer Redker, the community's treasurer, did not mince words. "It is hurting us. Sales tax revenues are not rising in light of our rising population," he said. "Without the 28,500 residents of Hoffman Estates, Woodfield could not exist...Why should Schaumburg get the money?" The paper noted that Hoffman Estates was netting approximately $18,000 to $20,000 per month, one-sixth of Schaumburg's take. Redker went as far as to propose, "I hope someone challenges this unfair tax to the Illinois Supreme Court, and it is overturned. Taxes of this kind should be divided equally among all of the state's communities." Mount Prospect finance director Richard Jesse echoed Redker's sentiments, noting that the village's gain in sales tax revenue was slowed by Woodfield, stating, "Tax revenues have not gone up the way we had hoped, based on our growth in previous years."

Others remained optimistic. The *Tribune* reported on shopping centers as far away (though geographically rather close) as Golf Mill in Niles. Albert A. Yort, the center's general manager, admitted, "We noticed a slight dip at first, but most of those from our area who went to Woodfield went as sightseers. Most of our regular costumers have reported back in, and any overall effect has been slight."

Still others were fearful. John O'Halloran, manager of Crawford's Department Store in Rolling Meadows, said bluntly, "There is no denying that Woodfield has made a big difference. We'd be crazy to deny it."

Meanwhile, Randhurst officials appeared unfazed, dismissing Woodfield as a fad. "Our projections indicate we will be back where we started by August, exactly a year after Woodfield opened," declared Randhurst manager Harold J. Carlson defiantly.[103] During the decade of the 1970s, shopping malls were popping up like weeds all over the burgeoning suburban communities of Chicago. What accounted for this unbridled growth in shopping centers?

A special in the *Chicago Tribune* in February 1973 specifically profiled the northwest suburbs. For the first time since the population booms of the 1950s and '60s, Mount Prospect and the surrounding communities were becoming self-contained. The article noted that the four-township area of northwest Chicago had already surpassed entire metropolitan areas such as Birmingham, Alabama, in population. Chicago transplants and Des Plaines residents the Topeczewski family were profiled. The family had moved from Chicago fifteen years earlier and, according to the paper, had no desire to move their four children back to the city under any circumstances. Mrs. Topeczewski bragged that the area now had everything the family needed that they used to find in Chicago and, moreover, lacked the negative aspects of the city:

> *We have big shopping centers, good restaurants, theaters—almost everything you can think of. The suburbs and the schools here offer so many more opportunities for the children than the city does. Chicago has so much pollution and traffic congestion. And I wouldn't like to walk in the Loop by myself anymore.*

Transition was the theme as the paper invited its readers to

> *take a meandering drive through the Northwest suburbs and you cross expanses of open land, some matted with the stubble of crops where farmers living in rickety houses are holding out for just a little more money from real estate developers. The transitions are abrupt—from desolation to areas of intense activity where bulldozers carve out the prairies and construction workers frame out buildings that seem to spring up overnight.*[104]

Louis H. Masotti, director of Northwestern University's Center for Urban Affairs, warned the *Tribune* that suburban areas, especially Chicago's northwest suburbs, could no longer be regarded as "isolated bedroom communities for organization men living in split-level traps. Suburbia was now 'the new America, the city of the '70s.'"[105] For its part, the newspaper was kind to Mount Prospect, describing it as "offer[ing] the well-settled feeling of the rail-road spine communities despite the flashy presence of Randhurst, the area's second largest shopping center [eighty-three stores in 1,030,000 square feet]."[106]

Urban historian Robert Fishman dubbed these communities "technoburbs." He explained:

> *By "technoburb," I mean a peripheral zone, perhaps as large as a county, that has emerged as a viable socio-economic unit. Spread out along its highway growth corridors are shopping malls, industrial parks, campuslike office complexes, hospitals, schools, and a full range of housing types. Its residents look to their immediate surroundings rather than the city for their jobs and other needs; and its industries find not only the employees they need but also the specialized services.*[107]

Moreover, the construction of shopping centers supported this claim. During this same period, less than a decade after Randhurst was built, it was reported that Chicagoland now contained thirteen regional shopping

Randhurst was also home to a number of regional police and fire shows. Seen here are two "hard-boiled," unidentified motorcycle officers from the Niles Police Department, circa 1963.

centers supporting over twelve hundred stores and fifteen million square feet of selling space.[108] These shopping centers had a ripple effect that also attracted offices, apartments, satellite centers of convenience food, drug and furniture stores, car dealerships, motels and single-family-home subdivisions. The now-legendary names of centers such as Lakehurst, Lincoln Mall and Yorktown were new to the Chicago-area lexicon in this period.

The early 1970s saw Randhurst celebrate its ninth anniversary with fanfare, no doubt to regain the spotlight after it had been upstaged by Woodfield and perhaps to remind shoppers that it was here first. The festivities included a full three-ring circus, featuring "aerialists, gymnasts, clowns, perch-pole balancers and a six-piece circus band." There were a whopping twenty-seven performances in less than two weeks, and the celebration climaxed in a fireworks display.[109]

The village also sought to fortify shopping at Randhurst during this trying period by reaching out to Chicago, announcing the addition of a bus line to the center from the Jefferson Park Chicago Transit Authority hub in March 1972. The costs were shared three ways by the Village of Mount Prospect, the Randhurst Corporation and United Motor Coach Company, which had originated the project. The route saw eight runs each way, Monday through Saturday, with the last run departing Randhurst at 3:00 p.m. because, as Randhurst manager Harold Carlson, always thinking of the automobile, noted, "It was felt fathers would be returning from work with the family car shortly after." The route was similar to a "Shoppers' Special" that had run the previous Christmas season.[110] The bus route did not have the desired effect, and by June 17, a mere three months after its inception, the program ceased operations, citing a "lack of enough riders to make the run self-sufficient." Mayor Robert D. Teichert echoed these sentiments, stating that the bus route "did not have a broad enough service base to be subsidized by Mount Prospect." Robert Eppley, the village manager, thought that part of the problem was that riding the bus was "not the fashionable thing." At any rate, the village claimed that the data provided by the bus route would be of use if the village attempted to determine whether public transportation within the village was necessary. A United Motor Coach official stated vaguely, "We still hope to do something someday."[111]

During the decade of the 1970s, Randhurst continued to use a variety of promotions and the construction of additional businesses to attract shoppers. A fixture of Randhurst in this decade was the construction of the Twin Ice Arena. The construction of the $1.5 million "sports center" complex was announced in late March 1972 by W.J. Marshall Jr., chairman of Metro

Sports, Inc., in an effort to build a nationwide network of ice hockey and tennis arenas.[112] The center was situated as an outparcel building on the southeast portion of the property and included two separate arenas—an ice-skating practice arena and a spectator arena containing two thousand permanent seats. The spectator arena would encompass 28,000 square feet and be used for "competitive meets, amateur hockey, figure skating and speed skating," while the practice arena, weighing in at 19,650 square feet and located just west of the spectator arena, would be use for "figure skating, skating instruction, hockey practices and minor hockey meets." Marshall told the *Mount Prospect Herald* that the sports center concept was intended to encourage amateur hockey and ice-skating programs but that the complex would provide a place for involvement in many indoor sports activities.

Even before it was built, the arena announced that it would be the home rink for six teams of the Chicago Minor Hawk Hockey Foundation and was entering into negotiations with the Chicago Figure Skating Association to make the Twin Ice Arena the organization's base of operations.[113] The first mentions of hockey teams to call the arena home appear in 1973. The Chicago Nordics, coached by former Blackhawk Ken Wharram, were the Chicago area's first venture into Junior "A" minor-league hockey.[114] By January 1, 1974, it was reported that the Chicago Cardinals of the North American Hockey Association would play an exhibition game against the reigning six-time Czechoslovakian team Dukla Jihlava, which had arrived from Bloomington, Minnesota, where they competed in the World Cup Tournament. *Chicago Tribune* sportswriter Bob Verdi noted, "Unlike the semi-pro Cardinals, who by the way are 15–0 this year, the Czechs play the game year-round. It's a job, and if they don't cut it, it's back to the mines or factory or newspaper office." Blackhawks great Stan Mikita, whom Verdi dubbed the "uncheckable Czech," commented, "Hockey is coming, it should be a good show."[115]

The Randhurst Twin Ice Arena gained continued notoriety in 1974 when it was the site of the *Chicago Tribune*'s Silver Skates Derbies, the paper's oldest sports promotion. The first Silver Skates was held in 1917 and been located previously in such sites as the Humboldt Park Lagoon, Waveland Park, Northbrook and Park Ridge, both indoors and outdoors. The "exciting, sparkling" indoor ice arena in Mount Prospect would also mark the first time the event was held in the northwest suburbs.[116] Several weeks later, the 1976 U.S. Olympic speed skating team was on display as the Amateur Speed Skating Association hosted the National Indoor Speed Skating Championships at Randhurst. Olympic champions and Northbrook residents Anne Henning and Diane Holum were on hand to present trophies.[117]

Despite all these events, Randhurst Twin Ice Arena will likely be best remembered, for better or worse, as the unwitting home of the Chicago Cougars Hockey Team. In the Cougars' short-lived, three-season existence, the 1973–4 season—and the arena itself—would capture the imagination of Chicago hockey fans. The Chicago Cougars were an original team in the World Hockey Association, established in 1972 as a professional league to rival the National Hockey League. The Cougars were to be seen as an anchor of the upstart league, given the popularity of the Chicago Blackhawks in the city. The owners of the team were successful Chicago restaurateurs Walter and Jordan Kaiser. Moreover, it appeared that the Cougars further tried to capitalize on the Blackhawks' popularity by waging an aggressive campaign to sign the team's players, including Bobby Hull.[118] The Cougars set up shop in the South Side's International Amphitheatre on the site of the infamous Chicago Stockyards. Four years earlier, the amphitheatre had been ground zero for the anti–Vietnam War movement as the venue for the 1968 Democratic Convention. At one time the country's largest indoor venue, the amphitheatre hosted countless rock concerts, including the Beatles, and numerous national trade shows.

The Cougars, despite their best efforts, were having difficulty filling the nine-thousand-seat auditorium. In its inaugural season, the team was also having difficulty finding a win, finishing its first season at a disastrous 26-50-2. Led by Captain Larry Cahan, who was known for his "chippy" play, the team finished at the bottom of the league in goals but at the top in penalty minutes.[119]

Needless to say, not too many residents were expecting much out of the Cougars. The year 1973 did see some key NHL pickups for the franchise, including Rosaire Paiement; center Ralph Backstrom, a six-time Stanley Cup champion from the Montreal Canadiens; and defensiveman Pat Stapleton, who had just finished eight seasons with the Blackhawks as the team's "little big man." Stapleton would also serve as the team's playing coach. While the Cougars' season was not overly impressive, they managed to finish 38-35-5 and, as a result, limped into the playoffs.[120]

The story would seemingly end here, as the Cougars faced the defending champion New England Whalers. However, in a grueling, full seven-game series, the Cougars emerged victorious. They would now go on to face the Toronto Toros, a well-established team in the WHA.[121]

There was one problem.

Given the Cougars' devastating opening season and the fact that virtually no one expected the team to land a playoff berth, let alone defeat the defending champions, the owners of the International Amphitheatre likely did not

Pat Stapleton, the longtime "little big man" of the Chicago Blackhawks who served as both the Cougars' coach and one of their star players, is seen in action.

think twice when they, months prior, booked a national touring production of *Peter Pan*, starring Olympic gymnast Cathy Rigby in the title role, to be featured at the theater. Thus, the amphitheatre would be unavailable to host the three Cougars home games of the seven-game playoff series. This aptly named "Peter Pan Incident" caused some in Chicago to take notice. *Tribune* reporter Art Dunn noted:

> *After two days of uncertainty about where the Chicago Cougars would call home for the second round of the World Hockey Association playoffs against the Toronto Toros, they decided late today to hang their sticks in the suburban shopping center…Next stop, Randhurst Twin Ice Arena in Mount Prospect.*[122]

The arena had twenty-five hundred permanent seats, which expanded to twenty-eight hundred with the use of portable bleachers. There was a six-day delay between games two and three because of, appropriately enough, an ice show booked at the Twin Ice Arena. Cougar president Walter Kaiser had been offered the use of arenas from as far as away as Vancouver and Springfield, Massachusetts. There was also talk of having the home games in Cleveland or at the University of Notre Dame in South Bend, Indiana. However, Kaiser was determined to host the home games in Chicago, stating, "We wanted to play in Chicago to accommodate our season ticket holders." According to the *Tribune*, the Cougars brass held out eleventh-hour hope of landing the Chicago Stadium, home of the Blackhawks, which contributed to the delay in the choice of Randhurst: "There are obvious scheduling difficulties in King Arthur's Madison Street Mint [Hawks, Bulls, Frank Sinatra], and besides the Stadium did not return any phone calls from the Cougars." The moniker of "King Arthur's Madison Street Mint" was a reference to the wealth and power of Arthur Wirtz and his family, who at the time owned the Chicago Bulls and Chicago Blackhawks and used his Chicago Stadium to attract the biggest musical acts of the day.

Kaiser quipped, "I seem to be one of the rare owners in Chicago who thinks about the fans," and added, "From a financial standpoint, playing in Randhurst will be disastrous." Adding insult to injury, the airport ground crews in Toronto were on strike, forcing the team to land in Buffalo and to be bused in to Canada. A defiant Pat Stapleton was undaunted, telling the *Tribune*, "What's the difference? We've got to win four games wherever we play." After the exhausting two-game series, they headed "home," tied 1-1.

By the time the team arrived home, the city was beginning to take notice. David Condon's *Tribune* column "In the Wake of the News" was devoted entirely to the Cougars. He stated, "You've got to hand it to the Brothers Kaiser for keeping playoffs in Chicago after the Peter Pan cast evicted 'em from the amphitheater." Discussing the debacle in finding a venue to host the Cougars, and his determination to keep the games in Chicago, Walter Kaiser commented to Condon about the possibility of the team playing at Notre Dame, admitting:

> *Sure, we could have gone to Notre Dame. In fact, Notre Dame's Convocation Center would have been our next choice if Randhurst hadn't been available. It'd have been an imposition to ask people to drive all that way. We're a Chicago team, not an Indiana team. Anyhow, at Randhurst we can accommodate all our season ticket holders. Of course, we've raised the price but it balances out if you consider that parking is free and there's no driving to South Bend.*

Condon noted that Kaiser was told that the representatives of the World Hockey Association "didn't even want the Cougars to consider Randhurst," to which Kaiser replied:

> *If we'd have promised Vancouver to play our semi-finals—and hopefully the finals—out there, they'd have guaranteed the Cougars more than 10,000*

> *attendance...I don't think we need make any apology. Performance tells the tale. We've never given up.*

A confident Kaiser ended the interview by stating, "As I see it, right now we're just about three players short of being an even match for the Blackhawks... or any team in hockey. Right now I'd like to project a championship for this season...It's still going on you know."[123]

Shortly afterward, in the *Tribune*'s annual Hockey Awards, the paper declared that the "Shame of the Year" was that the Cougars, "a team that deserves better, has to skate among the grocery carts of Randhurst." The paper asked rhetorically, "If they lick Toronto, can we call them the Chicago Green Stamps?"[124]

Game three of the series was played among the "heat and fog in the Randhurst Arena." Apparently, it was a rather brutal game, with the Toros losing two defensemen. One, Rick Cunningham, "stopped a Cougar shot with his foot" and suffered a badly swollen ankle. Much more seriously, Toro rearguard Steve Cuddie was struck in the face with a puck, which shattered the glass in his contact lens, and was taken to nearby Lutheran General Hospital in Park Ridge. In the end, the battered, "weary defensivemen" of the Toros were defeated by the Cougars 3–2 under the leadership of Rosaire Paiement, who scored his second and third playoff goals. The crowd gathered at Randhurst was just under capacity, and there was no doubt where their hockey loyalties lay. When it was announced that the Blackhawks, competing in National Hockey League playoffs, had been badly beaten by the Boston Bruins, the crowd "cheered lustily."[125]

As the city and the team braced for game four, Cougar fans were now able to react to the Randhurst Twin Ice Arena. Cougars fan Ward Melanger of Chicago declared facetiously, "I went out to Randhurst to see the Cougars play. I had to sit in a shopping cart. Twice they faced off in the coffee shop."[126]

Playing two games within twenty-four hours, game four was termed a "shooting gallery decision," won by the Toros at Randhurst, as was game five in Maple Leaf Gardens at Toronto, with the Toros again prevailing by a score of 5–3 in a game where "whistles were heard more often than cheers for hockey excellence." This left the series at a heated 3-2.[127] The *Tribune* reported that the

> *Indomitable Cougars, Chicago's last link to a long, long winter attempt to postpone sudden summer in Randhurst Twin Ice Arena. The team nobody wants skates onto the rink nobody believes in confronted with*

another win or else situation. The feisty Cats have faced it more often than a high roller in Vegas to achieve a place among the last six survivors in major league hockey.[128]

Game six was described as a "goring" and a "scoring orgy," in which the Cougars trounced the Toros 9–2 at Randhurst. While the victory was a huge boost for the team, the players were quick to dismiss it. Center Ralph Backstrom, the "combat-hardened veteran of playoff hockey," declared flatly, "We have to forget about this…It won't mean a thing unless we win." By this time, it was known that the winner of game seven would face the Houston Aeros, either in Toronto's Maple Leaf Garden or "wherever the Cougars decided to call home." The *Tribune* couldn't resist acknowledging the fact that the Houston Aeros had been on a long rest, due to the fact that *Peter Pan*, now a seemingly official WHA arch rival, was occupying Sam Houston Arena until May 12. Amazingly, the Cougars won the game and secured a spot in the championship series. Jordan Kaiser did not have time to celebrate with the team. After it was clear that the Cougars were poised to win the game, he scrambled to the press box in an attempt to secure a venue for the finals.

This also left many in Chicago wondering what the immediate future would hold for the team, with reporter Art Dunn asking, perhaps a bit backhandedly, after the Cougars beat out the Toros, now what? Dunn reported that if the Cougars were to take "this weird semi," they wouldn't be calling Chicago Stadium home. He noted the Kaiser brothers, whom he termed "pro hockey's version of Homer's Odyssey," were feeling quite jilted by the Chicago

Chicago Cougars team photo, taken during the 1973–4 season of their unlikely championship run.

authorities. "We just heard that the electricity was turned off and the ice defrosted in [Chicago] Stadium after the final Bruin-Blackhawk game," said a flustered Jordan Kaiser. "They've made sure we aren't going to play there." Jordan Kaiser even reached out to "Da Mare" Richard Daley himself, to no avail. "You would think Mayor Daley would want a Chicago team to play in Chicago…but apparently not." The article ended with a frantic plea to "everyone with an arena capable of holding major league finals," noting that "the WHA is not happy with Randhurst. It's just too small for a championship series which will be on national television." Kaiser told the paper that he had convinced President Murphy, for the sake of the fans, that Randhurst would do "in a pinch" but submitted that "it's just one more obstacle we'll have to overcome." Dunn, speaking of the heated rivalry between the leagues, noted humorously that according to the terms of a recent truce between the leagues, NHL teams could no longer prohibit WHA teams from using their facilities if the price was right, but as he noted, "The agreement says nothing about returning phone calls or when to defrost a sheet of ice."[129]

Despite the best efforts of the Kaiser brothers, and to the chagrin of President Murphy and the WHA brass, the *Tribune* announced that the Cougars would open the finals at where else but Randhurst Twin Ice Arena. The paper declared:

> *By process of elimination, the Chicago Cougars have opted to open the World Hockey Association title round…Sunday night in Randhurst Twin Ice Arena. You read it right. The very same shopping-center rink in Mount Prospect that only Monday was branded "unsuitable" by Dennis Murphy, W.H.A. president.*

The article quoted a despondent Walter Kaiser as lamenting, "Where else do I have to play? There's no ice in the amphitheatre and the Wirtzes [who owned the stadium and the NHL franchise therein] won't return our calls." Kaiser noted that the International Amphitheatre, the "home" of the Cougars, was now free of *Peter Pan*, but "there's a wrestling show in there Saturday night which can't be moved." Kaiser reiterated the fact that he was determined to keep his team in Chicago, stating, "Going back to Randhurst is the best decision for the fans." President Murphy was not as apologetic, citing the loss of television revenue and general lack of "prestige":

> *It's a shame to have to play in Randhurst…It's appalling to the league. But it's a compliment to the Kaisers to want to play in Chicago. There's no other*

Chicago Cougars 1973–4 West All-Stars Rosaire Paiement, Ralph Backstrom and Pat Stapleton are seen here exchanging pleasantries with an opponent from the East All-Star Team.

> *alternative. It's their decision to stay in Chicago, not mine...I'm going to get static from the other owners about having the finals in Randhurst...But the Kaisers deserve to choose their own destiny. The Cougars made the finals and they shouldn't be penalized by being forced out of town. The Kaisers are taking a big* [financial] *beating; I hope the fans appreciate it.*[130]

Randhurst, however, did have its defenders. The *Tribune* stated:

> *Many of the descriptive phrases uttered about the 3,000-seat rink can only be described as "expletive deleted." Putting people like...Pat Stapleton and Ralph Backstrom together in an amateur arena to scrap for the Avco World Trophy, it is generally felt, is like hanging Rembrandts in an outhouse.*

The newspaper noted that a prominent exception existed in the form of Cougar Rosaire Paiement, who had up to that point scored six goals in three playoff games at Randhurst. "It's been good for me here...and it's better to play in Randhurst than all over the place." While Randhurst was the topic of the Chicago sports headlines, the greater opponent would prove to be the Houston Aeros, whose star player was none other than "Mr. Hockey" himself, the legendary Gordie Howe. He was supported on the ice by two of his sons, Mark and Marty. This was when the proverbial glass slipper broke. Led by the Howe family, the Cougars were helplessly swept by the Aeros. Likely, the Cougars were not too hard on themselves for this loss, as the Aeros, under the Howes, would retain the championship the following season and were runners-up in the next. For his part, despite his innumerable accomplishments and contributions to professional hockey, Howe said of getting on the ice in a Houston Aeros uniform with his sons in 1973 at Randhurst Twin Ice Arena in front of a "crowd" of two thousand: "I always refer to that as my greatest accomplishment and excitement."[131]

While the Randhurst Twin Ice Arena was designed to host amateur hockey, its legacy will be forever entwined with some of hockey's greatest players. The arena also hosted some of rock and roll's most noted bands in the late 1970s, including Ted Nugent, Rush and Kansas. It was later converted into a Child World toy store. While the Twin Ice Arena did not last long, neither did the Chicago Cougars nor the World Hockey Association, for that matter. The Kaisers abandoned the team, and after a valiant effort by the players to salvage it, the Cougars disbanded after the 1974–5 season. The entire league would suffer the same fate soon after, collapsing after the 1978–9 season, with four franchises—the Edmonton Oilers, New England (later "Hartford") Whalers, Winnipeg Jets and Quebec Nordics—moving to the National Hockey League.

Despite the fanfare surrounding its tenth anniversary and the attention brought by the Chicago Cougars and various musical acts and mall promotions, Randhurst limped out of the 1970s significantly weakened

The Randhurst Twin Ice Arena is seen here after its conversion to a Child World toy store during the 1980s. This nondescript building hosted legends of both pro hockey and rock music throughout the 1970s.

by numerous massive competitors, which were only minutes away. On its tenth anniversary, Randhurst ran large ads in local papers featuring a large drawing of Randhurst's water tower, with the caption, "A Landmark for Shoppers." It told readers, somewhat defiantly, and with some shots across Woodfield's bow, that

> *since its opening 10 years ago, Randhurst and the familiar "R" atop its water tower have become synonymous with outstanding values and selections. Randhurst, the pioneer in totally enclosed major shopping centers, is still a leader in its field because of its unique triangular design, vast selection of fine stores and dedication to courteous service to all its customers. Randhurst customers enjoy the close-in easy parking and they know that once inside Randhurst, it takes a minimum amount of steps to go from one store to the other, making shopping at Randhurst a totally pleasant time-saving experience. Randhurst thanks its wonderful customers for 10 years of success and looks forward to serving them in the future.*[132]

This would certainly not be the last time Randhurst would offer itself as a "convenient" alternative to neighboring shopping centers, especially Woodfield.

Randhurst used its fifteenth anniversary in 1977 as an excuse to give the center even more attention, with the first of many major facelifts to the tune of $500,000. Manager Harold Carlson told the media:

> *When we opened in 1962, we were the first enclosed mall in the Chicago area and for a day or two, we were the world's largest mall...But 15 years is 15 years and we think it began to show its age. Modern merchandise should be displayed in a modern showcase...This may have been overdue.*

The remodeling would strip Randhurst of many of the architectural touches of Gruen. Carlson noted that the remodeling included replacing the original concrete floor with terrazzo, a covering of small marble chips set in concrete and polished; installing new light fixtures so real plants could replace artificial ones; hanging "soft sculptures" from the ceiling, which Carlson described as "three-dimensional fabric designs on different themes," with one section of the mall having a forest theme, one a sun sculpture and one a day-and-night design; and replacing the stone benches and trash cans. Carlson noted that the mall's decorative pools and fountains would be eliminated. He stated, "All the mall amenities will be semiportable so when

This photo of an appearance by talk radio pioneer Wally Phillips shows Randhurst's rather sterile remodeling during 1978. The "soft sculptures" can be partially seen in the top middle of the photo.

a display or exhibit comes around, we can rearrange things. This will give us a lot of flexibility." Additionally, the space-aged sprayed concrete on the ceiling of the center was covered with tile. Carlson further noted that mall hours would not be affected. He told the newspaper, "It looks like World War III on the mall right now, but people are putting up with the temporary mess. The merchants and customers seem to be excited." Carlson was also quick to point out that the remodeling was not sparked by declining revenue. He reassured the public, "In fact, business has been thriving. The only year in our history that business went down was the year Woodfield opened."[133]

A *Tribune* report in 1979 of active shopping centers in the Chicago market pointed out that Randhurst had plummeted to tenth on the list of most profitable centers in Chicagoland, while Woodfield remained king, taking in an estimated $305 million, out earning its nearest competitor by almost $100 million and Randhurst by nearly $200 million. The report saw the greatest percentage increases among newcomers Northbrook Court, Orland Square Mall and Water Tower Place, all constructed in 1976.[134] In what

Left: "I refuse to pay alimony for these bastard developments." Architect Victor Gruen came to denounce his own creations toward the end of his life. *Image provided by Victor Gruen Collection, American Heritage Center, University of Wyoming. Used with permission.*

Below: This aerial view of the greater Woodfield area is an example of what Gruen feared most about the excessive construction of shopping centers: sprawl.

Greater Woodfield Area / Woodfield Park Schaumburg, Illinois

WOODFIELD PARK is a 325-acre planned commercial develo
J. Emil Anderson & Son, Inc. Large and small tracts of land or
selective basis for build-to-suit offices, retail buildings, restau

could be seen as a metaphor for the reckless abandon of shopping center construction and its effect on Randhurst, in early January 1979, the roof of the Carson, Pirie, Scott & Co. store at Randhurst partially collapsed under the weight of a snowstorm. Fortunately, no one was injured.[135]

In the midst of a worldwide boom in shopping center construction, an aging Victor Gruen had begun to denounce his own creations. His centers, he claimed, were meant to be "more than selling machines," and he blamed "fast-buck promoters and speculators" for the out-of-control growth of malls and shopping centers.[136] In a final dismissal, he famously stated, "I refuse to pay alimony for these bastard developments."[137] Soon after, in 1980, the architect passed away in his beloved Vienna, disillusioned and resentful of the fact that suburban shopping centers had affected and altered even his native city.

As it had once come to be among the leading inventions and innovations of regional shopping centers, Randhurst was now poised to reinvent itself to meet the challenges of hyper-retailing in the technoburbs of the 1980s and would do so by abandoning many of Gruen's original design principles.

8

"Replacement May Be the Only Solution"

The Rouse Corporation and Randhurst in the 1980s

Confidential

Find enclosed for your information only a copy of the report recently submitted...on Randhurst proposed refurbishing. The items are not necessarily going to happen but I would hope that most of them will in the very near future.

It looks like we now have at least a better sense of direction as to what is needed, and this should help us in our efforts to lease the center and generate excitement.

Randhurst is a unique plan configuration which I suspect has lacked the flexibility to accommodate any significant expansion or to respond to diminishing store sizes over the years. However, I think the plan does have exciting possibilities.[138]

By the 1980s, Randhurst was feeling its age. Competing malls had dealt financial blows to Randhurst almost before its paint was dry, most notably nearby Woodfield. By 1981, the corporation, which had been touted as all but indestructible, harnessing the financial power of three of the Midwest's foremost department stores, had been dissolved. While Randhurst had undergone slight renovations in 1978, it continued to be one-upped at every turn by new shopping centers, which were now popping up all over the region. After two decades, what had originally made Randhurst new and exciting was now accused of making it dated, boring and ugly. The 1980s proved to be another watershed moment for Randhurst, as the center was again put in the hands of a giant of American commercial architecture. While the center would undergo many changes during this period, some of which were contrary to Gruen's original intentions, it could be argued that these changes were implemented for some of the same reasons that Victor Gruen planned in the 1960s, specifically to impress a new generation of "powers that be" in Chicago. The *Chicago Tribune* announced on May 21, 1981, that the Maryland-based Rouse Company had agreed to purchase Randhurst for an undisclosed sum.

By this time, the Rouse Company, much like Victor Gruen Associates two decades prior, was considered the nation's premier development firm. The story of Gruen and Rouse intertwines on many levels. Its founder, James W. Rouse, had at one time collaborated, quite successfully, with Gruen on Cherry Hill Shopping Center in Cherry Hill, New Jersey. The center, constructed in 1961, just before Randhurst, while not as grand as Randhurst, produced similar positive reactions from the public. Approximately 100,000 people visited the structure upon its opening, and five national magazines ran favorable articles. Rouse, whose own company was beginning to boom, wrote to Gruen on his seventieth birthday and told him glowingly, and perhaps much to Gruen's solace, "There is no space which we have produced that is as grand and floating as Cherry Court…I have always felt that you built it with your own hands." Rouse further told Gruen, "You touched me and my associates at an important point of time in our individual growth and in the growth of our company" and gave Gruen credit for rocketing his company from "the provinces to the bigtime."[139] Now, in a perfect twist of fate, one of Victor Gruen's gems was fully in the hands of the Rouse Company.

Shortly after the purchase of Randhurst, James W. Rouse appeared on the cover of *Time* magazine. By this time, Rouse had achieved what Victor Gruen was never able to do. He had revitalized the downtowns of major American cities. The article noted Rouse's highly successful "festive marketplaces," which had transformed decrepit portions of Boston, Philadelphia, Santa Monica and his own Baltimore into thriving public areas that blended commerce, entertainment and civic activities. One did not have to look far to see his inspiration. *Time* noted that

> *Rouse…considers himself a developer, but is best described as an urban visionary…he has shown a unique and uncanny ability to blend commerce and showmanship into a magnetizing force in the inner city. In the process, he has also sought to reshape current-day thinking about the functions and rewards of city life. The Rouse philosophy revolves not so much around*

> *real estate as around meeting the needs and desires of people…He has more than proved this point.*[140]

In a sentence, Rouse was truly able to please everyone. His massive projects incorporated historic buildings, made space for minority and locally owned businesses and even gave off an aura of hip places to be.[141]

The legacy of Rouse, when compared to his contemporary Gruen, is ironic, especially in the context of Randhurst. Gruen did so much to develop downtowns and inner cities but was remembered for his work on suburban shopping centers. Rouse, while credited with coining the term "shopping mall" and redesigning shopping centers such as Randhurst, was eulogized as the savior of decrepit downtowns. One could argue that because Gruen had put so much on the line to promote his shopping centers, Rouse was able to see Gruen-esque projects come to fruition. In the same way that one can compare, contrast and critique artists by looking at their respective works, the redevelopment of Randhurst serves as an interesting canvas for the similarities, and also vast differences, between Gruen and Rouse.

It would also appear that in the same way that Gruen had hoped to impress Chicago city officials with the success of Randhurst in order to get his chance to revitalize State Street, the Rouse Company, at the time of its purchase of Randhurst, was negotiating with city officials to work its magic on a downtown relic that was quickly becoming an eyesore: Navy Pier. However, before this could be accomplished, all eyes were, again, on Randhurst.

The *Chicago Tribune* reported in late 1983 that the shopping center was dolling up to recapture its lost customers.[142] The newspaper was able to sum up the rivalry between Randhurst and Woodfield quite succinctly, proclaiming in its opening sentence, "Watch out, Woodfield Mall, Randhurst wants it shoppers back." The paper went on to report that the aim in the renovation was to attract "active, young fashion followers who've passed by the Mt. Prospect shopping center to buy from its newer competitor malls in the northwest suburbs." The Rouse Company was radiantly described as "the fairy godmother of mall management firms…best known for its Cinderella transformations of deteriorated downtowns." The paper also noted that Rouse had proposed a similar treatment for Chicago's Navy Pier. Randhurst was Rouse's first entry into the Chicago market and was, during this period, known as "Rouse-Randhurst Shopping Center."

The renovations Rouse implemented borrowed heavily from the company's aforementioned "festive marketplaces," and in line with Rouse's personal egalitarian philosophies that local shops should get a crack at regional retailing, they set aside one-quarter of the stores for mom-and-pop operations.[143] The entire project was one of "visual accessibility," which opened up all areas of the mall, both literally and figuratively. In addition to physically opening up the center of the mall to the shopper, Randhurst's public spaces were all but eliminated in favor of retail expansion.[144]

Before this could be accomplished, there was a laundry list of items that had to be remedied in the center. Despite what was seen as the breathtakingly modern design of Randhurst upon its opening, many of its decorative elements were lambasted by a Rouse Company intra-office memorandum. The charges, some of which would have no doubt insulted Gruen, included:

> *The architecture, except for the roof dome, is undistinguished but satisfactory since it is predominantly brown brick uncluttered by tenant signs or other adverse visual elements. Unfortunately, additions to the Mall adjacent to the department stores have not used the same brick.*
>
> *The interior is in good repair but the all white color scheme with a cream color terrazzo floor has an institutional quality that needs to be changed to reflect the appearance of our newer centers.*
>
> *The acoustic plaster ceilings have a patched appearance and look dirty despite recent repainting. Replacement may be the only solution.*
>
> *Many of the storefronts look old and dated and need replacing to reinstate the Mall's fashionable image.*
>
> *Several tenants have internally illuminated signs featuring white plastic backgrounds which look dated, cheap (strip center image!), and emit considerable glare.*
>
> *Mall furniture: Replace movable backless benches (cheap looking).*
>
> *The three large triangular mall spaces between the dome and the department stores have no natural light, are oversize, empty and have no amenities, yet they represent the main mall in this unique shopping center plan. Consequently, they require the most substantial changes to achieve a satisfactory refurbishing solution commensurate in quality with the remainder of the center.*
>
> *Consider replacing the upper level offices with retail tenants and installing a pair of escalators. This would accommodate the small tenants that are not presently in the mall because of the excessive store depth (elevator access already exists).*
>
> *Remove the "artwork screens" around the clerestory (very dated).*
>
> *Lerner's is the wrong tenant for the most prominent space in the center! This space should be recaptured and leased as a café (the mechanical*

services already exist) or just made into a seating area with tables, chairs, ficus trees in terra cotta pots and a small "birdbath" fountain.

Remove the seal sculpture in Wards court and discard (ugly). Retain the penguin sculpture, have it re-bronzed and locate in one of the proposed pools.

The shingle roofs over the storefronts are as incongruous a feature as is imaginable in this space and should be replaced with a simple drywall proscenium the same as the House of Vision. The tenant signs around this Pavilion are poor designs and need replacing here particularly, because of their prominence.

In many ways, the improvements recommended to restore Randhurst's "fashionable image" may have pleased Gruen, but the largest one would have horrified him. There was little room for anything else in Randhurst other than retail. Even the pay phones and lockers would have to be removed from the center in the name of more retail space. Escalators, glass elevators

The Rouse Corporation lambasted the placement of Lerner's beneath the dome. Also note the "institutional" terrazzo floors that replaced Gruen's rustic polished concrete.

and pedestrian bridges saw to it that shoppers were able to access this new onslaught of retail as quickly as possible. The vital public spaces that Gruen had demanded of his centers were ripped from memory.

The Rouse Company was also among the first to introduce another concept to the Chicago area: an open seating area surrounded by a ring of fast-food vendors. This new-fangled concept was known informally as a "food court." It was to be the star of the Rouse renovation. In a shaky economy, it boasted the creation of 500 construction and 225 permanent jobs. The company's description of the new "monumental landmark" under the dome was enticing and likely would have garnered the approval of Victor Gruen himself. The area was dubbed "The Picnic" and assured customers that "the park-like atmosphere offers shoppers a relaxed area to enjoy a snack or meal...In addition to a unique assortment of eateries, the ambience of 'The Picnic' is delightful and pleasant, featuring skylights, glitter lighting and a look of clean, crisp tile." The Picnic occupied 7,715 square feet and would seat five hundred patrons. Restaurants featured would become local food court favorites as other shopping centers in the area followed Randhurst's lead. Their names (which were early examples of the delightfully kitschy business names that have come to define, for better or worse, our pictures of malls) and descriptions were, appropriately, varied and quite festive. This was, of course, in line with the Rouse Company philosophy:

> *Bananas—Fresh fruit cups and all-natural low-calorie frosty fruit shakes. Bon Appétit—Delicious homemade soups, salads and breads. Boardwalk Fries—Irresistible fresh cut potatoes. Café Bar—Assorted alcoholic drinks, authentic espresso and cappuccino. Diamond Dave's—Zesty, complete Mexican menu. Everything Yogurt—Tasty frozen yogurt in several flavors. Famous Gyros—Flavorful Greek sandwiches, salads and fine Baklava pastry. Hot Dogs & More—Specialty gourmet hot dogs. Manchu Wok—Tempting egg rolls and combination plates. McDonald's—Favorite menu of hamburgers. Pizzazz—Great Italian food with daily special. 1 Potato 2—Spectacular baked potatoes with choice of toppings. Skolnicks—Taste-tempting bagels, soups and bagel specialties. Swenson's—Gourmet ice cream.*[145]

The climax of the renovation occurred, as it had twenty-two years earlier, on a Thursday. Mount Prospect mayor and future state representative Carolyn Krause welcomed guests for a grand-reopening ceremony at 11:30 a.m. on October 4, 1984, along with the Prospect High School Band and

The centerpiece of Randhurst, literally and figuratively, during the 1980s was The Picnic food court, one of Chicagoland's first. While the center did away with many of the civic aspects of Gruen's design, it restored some aesthetic integrity.

Choir. About that same time, a drawing for a $1,000 shopping spree was conducted by the host of a hot new daytime show called *A.M. Chicago*, which was sweeping its competitors and making its charming host a rising star. Her name: Oprah Winfrey. Despite the countless retail incentives that day, Ms. Winfrey's $1,000 honorarium and transportation expenses for her two-hour appearance were, in hindsight, likely the biggest bargain of the grand reopening.[146] The day continued with a dizzying and colorful procession of "mimes, clowns, storybook characters, and violin quartets."

Claude LaMontagne, a thirteen-year Rouse veteran and new vice-president and general manager of Randhurst, addressed the crowd before the festivities began, making no secret of what the new Randhurst would provide to the community:

> *As you know, Randhurst has been around for a long time, but in the last year or so, this fine Center has seen more changes than it has in the previous twenty. A new generation is about to begin. New stores, more stores, and better stores are here—All dedicated to better serving the needs of our*

A.M. Chicago host and rising television star Oprah Winfrey helped to kick off the grand opening of Rouse-Randhurst's The Picnic food court in 1984.

customers. Dozens of dedicated people, through imagination, creativity and hard work made it happen. One of our corporate goals is, "To improve the physical environment and the quality of urban life available to people in the United States." With this goal in mind, we look at each project as a new creation. Jim Rouse, the founder of the company, summed up the process as follows: "It begins with the conviction that what we do is of enormous importance, that the lives of people and communities will be affected by it for generations to come, that the surest road to success in our venture is to discover the authentic needs and yearnings of people and do our best to serve them. It believes that people seek warm and human places with diversity and choice. It is a way of thinking that respects people; knows they care; believes everything matters; and knows that all details are important." This morning, the results are before you, and I am very honored to present Mount Prospect the new Randhurst with its exciting new Picnic Area.

While the speech was perhaps a bit lofty for the opening of a food court, it is telling of the "authentic needs" of northwest suburbanites during this period: retail, retail, retail. The national economy was on an upswing, and the historically strong buying power of the northwest suburbs was again beginning to awaken.

That weekend, a gala grand-opening fundraiser for the benefit of the March of Dimes would be held at the center. The shiny new "mall," as it was popularly called for the first time, was lit up until midnight to accommodate hundreds of guests and a slew of national and local celebrities, including former Chicago Cubs Jose Cardenal and Randy Hundley; former Chicago Bear Doug Buffone; Minnie Minoso and Dave Nelson of the Chicago White Sox; and former Blackhawk Dennis Hull. The glitterati also included *All My Children* star Richard Shoberg, who portrayed Tom Cudhay and fashion designer Babacho, in addition to Chicago radio personalities John Fisher, Doc Duncan, Don Wade and Greg Brown. The evening saw three bands perform in each major department store's court and a string quartet under the dome, where guests enjoyed an open bar and food catered by, fittingly, tenants of The Picnic. Guests were also treated to a "razzle-dazzle" fashion show highlighting the couture of the trendy new mall.[147] The expanded center now contained fifty new stores, including two new anchor stores, Joseph Spiess and MainStreet.[148]

As it was in 1962, the remainder of October was laden with promotions and entertainment, at least one event every single day until the end of the month. After the festivities died down, the real magic began. The Rouse Company's efforts worked their expected charm on the center, as well as the community. The renovation of Randhurst was credited with boosting the village's sales tax revenue to a thirteen-year high (the best since the opening of Woodfield Mall) and had a ripple effect that resulted in the revamping of the entirety of Mount Prospect. Randhurst was back.[149]

Like it had in 1962, change began to affect the new Randhurst almost immediately after its redevelopment. As America strode confidently into the 1990s, Randhurst was managing to keep pace with changing times, and in many cases, these changes were unforeseen. As the *Daily Herald* noted in the 1980s, "Management has been forced to think on its feet after running into some surprises not covered on any blueprints." The first of these "surprises" occurred in 1986, when original Randhurst anchor and Chicago staple Wieboldt's filed for bankruptcy and subsequently vacated its 209,000-square-foot store at the center. Fortunately, Rouse was able to avert disaster and scrambled to get P.A. Bergner into the space. Two years later, in 1988, one of the new anchors, the aforementioned MainStreet Department Store, was sold off by its parent company and became Kohl's

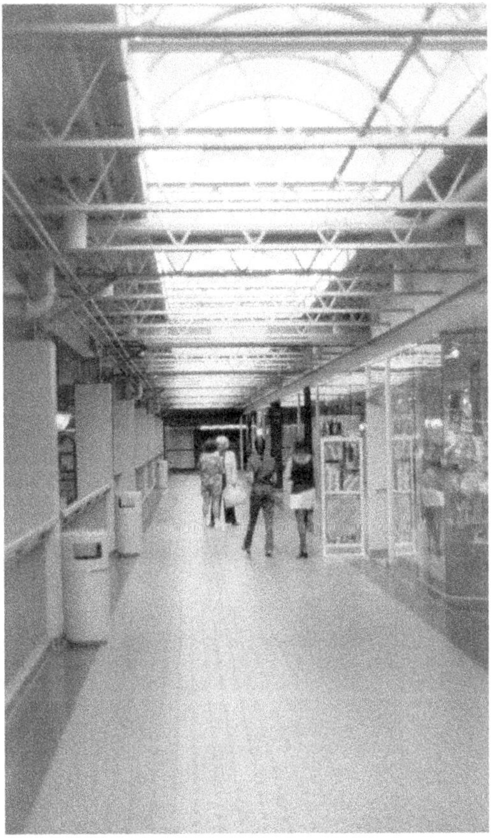

Above: Another rising star, NBA legend Michael "Air" Jordan, visited Randhurst during the mid-1980s to sign autographs for Chicago Bulls fans.

Right: Randhurst's "mysterious second level" of professional offices was converted into specialty shops in the late 1980s. Skylights and second-story anchor entrances were also added.

Department Store. Early in 1989, longtime tenant Chas A. Stevens folded but was partially replaced by Madigan's.[150]

As if these challenges were not enough, Rouse, astonishingly, announced that it would expand the center again in 1989. The offices of what Dave Aldrich termed "the mysterious second level" became fifteen "specialty shops," which would carry "fashion items such as women's clothing, jewelry and accessories."[151] Besides the specialty shops, the new "Upper Level Center Court," as it was dubbed, installed additional skylights, two new escalators, three walkways emerging from The Picnic to the second level and one other interesting feature. For the first time in its nearly thirty-year history, shoppers could now access the two-story anchor stores from the second level, now a staple of modern malls. As Randhurst never missed a chance for self-promotion, the opening of the improvements drew great fanfare. The *Mount Prospect Times* reported on these festivities, which occurred on, of all days, a Thursday, November 16, 1989. They featured the Prospect High School Marching Knights playing a stirring rendition of "Stars and Stripes Forever," a gigantic balloon drop and Dr. Tony Jones from TV's *General Hospital* serving free cake to shoppers. Mayor Gerald L. "Skip" Farley welcomed the expansion, calling Randhurst a "good corporate neighbor" and praising the developments as creating the feeling of a "real town center." He proudly announced to the onlookers, "More and more, as I'm about the village, I hear people say 'I do my shopping at Randhurst.'"[152] Rouse executive Peter Gruber seconded Farley's notion, telling the *Daily Herald*, "I think this project shows that Randhurst's pulse is rapid and heartbeat is good."

9

"The 'Grand Experiment' in the Bottom-Line World of High-Stakes Retailing"

Randhurst in the 1990s and 2000s

Randhurst Shopping Center in Mount Prospect, the largest enclosed mall in the world when it was built, is celebrating its 30th birthday today. And in the bottom-line world of high-stakes retailing, that has to be considered quite an accomplishment. Retailing is a stormy sea that could have sunk a lesser ship. Once the only kid on the block for shopping-starved residents of the burgeoning suburbs, Randhurst now is surrounded by competitors. But Randhurst has managed to sail through the storms and negotiate troubled waters many times through its 30 years, growing stronger each time as it battled changing merchandising trends, store closings and recessions.

Though sounding more like a eulogy, this reassuring description of Randhurst flew off the pages in an August 1992 special section of the *Daily Herald*. The country, as the newspaper hinted, was trudging through a recession. Randhurst was feeling the pinch; the *Herald* not only assured its readers that Randhurst would "sail through the storm," but it also took time to reflect on the structure's history. Some of the early shapers of Randhurst were now able to look back proudly, content in the notion that history had proved them right. Former chairman of Carson, Pirie, Scott & Co. and Randhurst vice-president and general manager Harold Spurway proudly told the paper from his retirement home in Florida that the construction of Randhurst was love at first sight:

> *It was a grand experiment...As soon as I saw the property, I knew I was interested. This area was red-hot and ready for development. We immediately saw the possibility of the growth and the access of the site to the whole region.*

"It was a real breakthrough," echoed John Lehrer, who was the original mind behind the early, albeit creative, promotional activities of the center. By 1992, his upstart firm was still headquartered at Randhurst and was serving clients throughout the country and the world. Lehrer was speaking of the center's triangular design, stating that it was responsible for "more exposure for the stores and less walking for customers."

Gruen himself also heralded the design of Randhurst. In his book, *The Heart of our Cities*, written shortly after the completion of the center, Gruen went as far as to cite Randhurst as a premier example of a pedestrian shopping center:

> *Randhurst Center, in Mount Prospect, near Chicago, "the largest shopping center under one roof," was opened in 1962. It contains three department stores which jointly own and operate the shopping center. Its building group is arranged with extreme compactness...It has abandoned those last vestiges of the former highway store: entrances and show windows of individual stores directed toward the parking area. (The department stores form the only exceptions in this respect.) Otherwise Randhurst represents one large ring of buildings surrounding a hexagonal, domed court, which is entered through three pedestrian arcades from the parking area.*[153]

The original vice-president and general manager of Randhurst, George M. O'Neill, was also able to reflect on Randhurst's grandeur and echoed Gruen's original ideas and intentions for his shopping centers, describing Randhurst as "a new downtown." "No expense was spared," O'Neill told the *Daily Herald* in 1987. "We really went overboard to do it right. The idea was to make it the center of civic activity—to transform an area like Mount Prospect into a downtown area."[154]

While sentiment and nostalgia were at a fever pitch for its history, the 1990s were turbulent for Randhurst. A roller-coaster ride of bankruptcies, store closings and competition characterized this decade. All the while, Randhurst remained resilient. By the time of its twenty-fifth anniversary, Randhurst was holding the line. Some of the retailers that saved Randhurst and allowed for several expansions in the late 1980s didn't last long themselves. The Child World that occupied the Randhurst Twin Ice Arena folded in early 1992. Madigan's, which had replaced Chas A. Stevens, closed in 1990, and recently built anchor Joseph Spiess closed in January 1992 after a $5 million facelift. The Carson's and Bergner stores, though bearing different names, now belonged to the same parent company, and thus the company renamed the Bergner's store Carson's and closed the original Carson's space. While this could have spelled doom for the center, Randhurst was able to bounce back. J.C. Penney moved into the original Carson's space in October 1990. The Madigan's space was divided between five tenants. A major women's retailer, Filene's Basement, probably known best as the site of the infamous "Running of the Brides" wedding dress sale, was also set to locate in, appropriately, the lower level of the center. The *Daily Herald* marveled, "Randhurst just won't give up."[155]

Manager Scott Ball commented on the changes that were hitting Randhurst and the new approaches the company was taking:

> *It's still going to matter most what you're selling in your store. What has changed for us, though, is that it's not enough to get the latest and greatest store in your center. You've definitely got to look closer at the financials of a prospective tenant. Before it was more of a merchandising decision.*

Ball concluded optimistically, "We've tried to take a tough situation and turn it into a positive. And besides, if you never have turnover, you can get stagnant."[156]

By the mid-1990s, things were again looking up for Randhurst. The center was now larger than ever and had swollen to five anchor stores, including Carson's, Montgomery Ward's, J.C. Penney, Kohl's (formerly MainStreet) and newcomers Circuit City and Old Navy, which split the space formerly occupied by Spiess. The defunct Child World was torn down and replaced by a Home Depot, which opened in the fall of 1995. The Jewel/Osco Store, which had left the center in 1970 for a freestanding out-lot store, was torn down and enlarged in the spring of 1996. During this time, the center also welcomed Waldenbooks, Frederick's of Hollywood, Great Clips and Cinnabon. Throughout the 1990s, Randhurst appeared to constantly reinvent itself. Instead of trying to outdo competitors, most notably Woodfield, it began billing itself as the "convenient" place to shop. General Manager Tom Shanley told the *Herald* in 1995 that the additions would "reinforce Randhurst's identity as a value- and convenience-oriented mall," admitting that Woodfield's "market area is much larger, but people don't visit so often. We will get a number of visits each month from people in our primary market."[157] These sentiments were echoed by *Daily Herald* staff writer Erin Holmes, who noted, "From the times when Randhurst Mall ruled as the only shopping center in the Northwest suburbs, to the pool of patrons it shares today with Schaumburg's Woodfield Mall, it's always had convenience on its side." She quoted Randhurst management as openly challenging its largest competitor: "We offer accessibility that probably isn't there for Woodfield. We offer convenience."[158]

Holmes also noted that Randhurst was holding strong because of its community partnerships with local schools, senior organizations and scouting groups. It also became a mecca for a new type of mall visitor. By 1997, Randhurst was keeping pace with Woodfield in this one demographic: the mall walker. The *Daily Herald* reported that Randhurst held the second-highest membership of mall walkers, at 775, just below Woodfield's 900.

All of these additions again worked their magic, and the center reported an "eye-popping" 40 percent jump in total sales in 1996.[159]

Sadly, the good news would, again, be short-lived. As Mount Prospect and the nation looked to the new millennium, Randhurst was again rocked by the loss of major tenants. After over a century in Chicago retailing, Montgomery Ward filed for bankruptcy in 2000 and closed its doors at Randhurst in June 2001. J.C. Penney smelled blood in the water and abandoned its anchor store just a few weeks later. Shortly afterward, Circuit City closed its Randhurst location, and Kohl's fled the center for a stand-alone location in southern Mount Prospect, while Old Navy moved to Arlington Heights.

Randhurst, though up against the ropes, received a ringing endorsement from *Daily Herald* columnist Jean Murphy when she confessed in her column, "It's OK to love a mall, especially Randhurst." In early 2002, after the departure of major anchors, Murphy told her readers:

> *It seems unfashionable to say these days, but I love Randhurst Mall. It is so close and convenient for a quick dinner on days I don't want to cook; for the new shoes my son just has to have, now; for birthday gifts; the new towels we desperately need; and even for a good book.*

Murphy reminded her readers of the large tax contribution that Randhurst contributed to village coffers, a whopping $2.9 million in 2000. She urged Mount Prospect residents to "quit talking about how Randhurst is becoming a 'ghost town' and patronize the remaining stores. Quit driving to Woodfield and Old Orchard to spend your money. There are plenty of nice things to buy at Randhurst."

Even the beloved Randhurst water tower was not without change. In an article cleverly titled "H2Oh!" the *Daily Herald* playfully told its readers:

> *Lime green? No, that doesn't quite describe it. Split pea? Mmm, yes, with chartreuse highlights. If you can imagine that. The color has been shocking drivers along Rand and Elmhurst roads in Mount Prospect for weeks. They startle when they approach Randhurst Shopping Center, where The Green has been slapped on a water tower that rises 145 feet high. Shoppers didn't know whether to call it the Grinch, the Incredible Hulk or a dill pickle. Mercifully, and before panic could ensue, workers finally started painting pretty prairie flowers in soft colors on the bulb at the top. "It's part of our new graphics and signage program," Lisa Blaszinski, marketing manager for the mall told the paper reassuringly. "It announces the Randhurst brand."*[160]

The water tower was part of a concentrated effort to give Randhurst a new look, and by default, a new appeal. "We are trying to create a landmark here," said Robert Cohen, regional manager of Randhurst. Mount Prospect Zoning Board member Leo Floros admitted, "We've been in the doldrums for so long at Randhurst," even going as far as to declare, "It's been an eyesore." In addition to the painting of the water tower, the company sought to incorporate vinyl signs with the action words: "Shop, Play, Dine."[161]

Despite this mass exodus from Randhurst, several bright spots appeared in the 2000s, the largest being the addition of a Costco Wholesale Warehouse. Costco was able to attract many customers back to Randhurst, but it had one feature that hurt the center itself: it was not attached to the mall. George Rosenbaum, chairman of Chicago-based retail marketing research firm Leo J. Shapiro and Associates, bluntly told a *Daily Herald* staff writer just before the center's forty-first birthday, "Randhurst probably saved itself by getting Costco…But they still need to find a mix of retailers inside the mall that can draw customers. Costco won't necessarily lend itself to cross-shopping."[162] Furthermore, all of the successful businesses that appeared in this period were outlying stores. Buffalo Wild Wings, another outparcel, reported the strongest opening numbers in its company history at the Randhurst location.

During this time, the departure of another longtime fixture at Randhurst occurred. After nearly two decades, the management of the mall went from the Rouse Corporation to Chicago-based Urban Retail Properties. These developers used the vacant space left by the anchors to experiment with a new type of shopping center, the open-air "lifestyle center." The plans called

Among the improvements made to Randhurst in the 1990s was the addition of this entrance archway.

for a Main Street–style promenade with outdoor access to small boutique shops, which would serve as a "grand entrance" to the interior of the mall.

The addition of Costco, the painting of the water tower and the addition of the promenade entrance were all part of what was being described as a national trend away from traditional mall construction, as shopping centers such as Randhurst looked for new ways to fill space vacated by department stores. John Melaniphy III, executive vice-president of Chicago-based consulting firm Melaniphy and Associates, noted, "The decline of traditional department stores has changed the way malls do business. You're seeing malls add open-air components that mimic an urban Main Street. We refer to it as a 'mall without a hall.'"[163] Urban Retail Properties' Michael Levin, citing nearby open-air malls Oakbrook Center and Old Orchard, was also sensing the change in sentiment, stating, "In the past, Randhurst's entrances have been blocked by the big department stores, and traditional malls often look dull from the outside. With the new entrance and the storefronts facing out, we'll have a much more inviting and attractive focal point."[164]

While it was decided that the enclosed portion of Randhurst would remain, these attitudes would soon spell doom for the mall. The entire superstructure would soon face demolition in favor of prevailing attitudes toward the Main Street lifestyle centers. The sentence was handed down early in 2007, when

Randhurst general manager Tom Castagnoli proposed the idea, "geared toward outdoor shopping with a combination of updated retail spaces and an increased amount of restaurant and entertainment opportunities," to the Village of Mount Prospect's Economic Development Commission.

The *Daily Herald* introduced its readers to the concept of a lifestyle center shortly after the proposal was made: "Sometimes referred to as 'boutique malls,' lifestyle centers are generally aimed at upscale customers and tailored to quick shopping trips, with convenient parking and attractive streetscapes."[165]

The newspaper noted that "Randhurst has the dubious distinction of being featured on www.deadmalls.com." By 2007, the interior of the mall had what the *Herald* termed as "interesting shops, but far from a retail hub." The newspaper reported that "out-parcels are Borders, Home Depot, Jewel, AMC Theaters and Buffalo Wild Wings. Anchors are Costco, Carson Pirie Scott, Steve & Barry's and Bed, Bath & Beyond. Those, at least, appear to be thriving." While officials from Randhurst and the Village of Mount Prospect made no promises about the future plans (Castagnoli told the *Herald*, "We're just dating the idea. We haven't married it yet."),[166] Randhurst's fate was sealed. In August 2008, the Mount Prospect Village Board voted unanimously to approve a $150 million development agreement that would gut the mall, announced just after Randhurst turned forty-six. Longtime Mount Prospect resident and village trustee John Korn echoed what were very likely the bittersweet feelings of many residents: "This is a historical event. Randhurst reminds me of that new car you loved when it was new, but as it aged and you had to put more money into it, there came a time to replace it."[167]

Randhurst Shopping Center closed its doors to the public for the last time on September 30, 2008. "A fond farewell for Randhurst" was the *Mount Prospect Times*' story of the year at the close of 2008:

> *It was last year's top story, and it may continue to be every year through 2010, when it reopens. That is how significant Randhurst Shopping Center was to Mount Prospect. Randhurst closed its doors for the last time on Sept. 30. Some folks fought back tears, others let a few slip while touring the building for the last time. In its final hours, young and old brought cameras and camcorders to preserve the images of a structure whose design has passed its time. Its decline turned a community landmark into an empty shell, but that shell will be torn down in 2009 and should spring to new life the year after that. Village Hall is awaiting the promise of new revenue; the state is considering how it will handle traffic at the nightmarish*

The "monumental landmark" that was Randhurst's dome looms eerily in the days leading up to its demolition. *Photo courtesy of Jim Conroy/Casto Lifestyle Properties.*

> *intersection; and shoppers across the Northwest suburbs* [wait to hear] *what stores will be opening there.*[168]

No doubt, the loss of Randhurst was a blow to many of Mount Prospect's residents, old and young. Like the places they live, work and worship, the place they shopped was undoubtedly an intimate and meaningful part of the residents' identity. However, in a tough economic climate in which the village and its residents depend on the tax revenues from the retail center that is, or was, Randhurst, there was certainly an overtone of optimism to the twinge of sadness that accompanied its demise. As Randhurst general manager Tom Castagnoli vowed to *Herald* readers: "If it all comes together, it's going to be a beautiful home run for Mount Prospect."[169]

Epilogue
"The Only Thing Constant in the Retailing Industry Is Change"

When I arrived in Mount Prospect in July 2008, a visit to Randhurst was one of my first trips. It had all of the symptoms of a dead mall: sparsely spaced stores, many of which appeared to be mom and pop; very few shoppers; and an overall feel of desolation. The carousel, which was placed underneath the dome to replace the Picnic about 2004, ran eerily in the relative silence. Even though it was my first visit, and by that time the center was rendered unimpressive, there was certainly a sense of history—this place had stories to tell us about how we live and, most especially, why we shop.

I have always likened my relationship to Randhurst to that of a recently deceased distant relative, the kind you never really knew too well when they were here, but after they've gone and you look through their possessions, you wish you had gotten to know them better. However, I do not see this book as an obituary to Randhurst; rather, it is a celebration of one of its many milestones.

As I wrap up the writing of this book, the community of Mount Prospect looks forward to another Randhurst Grand Opening, courtesy of Casto Lifestyle Properties, the center's current manager and itself a historic pioneer in shopping center development. As details of the tenants become available, the public looks forward to welcoming Randhurst Village and the benefits it will provide to Mount Prospect. In the midst of yet another severe economic downturn, Randhurst Village cannot arrive a day too soon. At the time this book went to press, the AMC Theater was nearing completion and preparing for grand opening in April 2011, and many upscale and trendy tenants such as Pei Wei Asian Diner, as well as the Billy Goat Tavern, a Chicago institution, were announcing their inclusion in the center. Needless to say, it was sad for many residents to see the majority of the mall lost to the wrecking ball. The demolition of the dome proved to be a final, and fitting, way for Randhurst to command attention one last time.

On an overcast, damp Friday morning, a group of village officials and spectators watched with cameras in hand as sparks flew from the massive iron supports that were being cut with torch welders. Large chains were attached to the dome and hooked up to large earth movers, which fired up their engines and lumbered away in opposite directions. In an instant, the dome slid from its supports and pancaked to the earth, shaking the ground beneath our feet. After several seconds, drops of mud flew down from the sky, as the dust rose from beneath the dome. A bittersweet end to a monumental landmark.

I hope this book offers some consolation and a chance to reflect on collective memories of Randhurst Shopping Center. To echo the quotation above, change has been a constant companion of Randhurst as it approaches its fiftieth year. It has changed to meet the challenges of retailing since its first days of operations, and Randhurst Village will be no exception.

Randhurst was not the first mall ever built, but I would argue that, for its time, it was the grandest and that it set the tone, or opened the floodgates,

Image courtesy of Casto Lifestyle Properties.

Before and after: two overhead views of Randhurst, including an architect's rendering of Randhurst Village. Casto Lifestyle Properties, while completely redesigning the center, has respected the center's historic legacy by keeping the "Randhurst" name and, as seen in this rendering, acknowledging the site of the dome in the open-air configuration.

for the massive shopping centers we know today. The combination of three retailers, the level of detail, the size and the ornate features of this elegant era make Randhurst a stand-alone shopping center. It also has the unique status of being one of the few shopping centers in existence that has, for better or worse, experienced virtually every aspect of "mallhood": pioneer, titan, squeezed-out competitor, dead mall and, again, the trendy new kid on the block.

What challenges and changes will Randhurst face in the "bottom-line world of high-stakes retailing" of the next half century? I don't know, but I'm sure it will be there to find out.

Like virtually every book that has ever been written, this, too, has been a labor of love. It is my first book, and in that spirit, I close by quoting Randhurst's original marketing coordinator, John Lehrer, when he reminisced about the center: "It's like the first automobile, the first airplane. It rivals that in uniqueness."

Thanks for reading.

Appendix A

Where Are They Now? A Guide to Selected Shopping Centers of Chicagoland

Market Square (1916): Though still a topic of debate, Lake Forest's Market Square is considered by some to be the first shopping center ever built. The argument is lent a good amount of credence by the fact that Market Square, which, astonishingly, is still standing, was designated on the National Register of Historic Places in 1979 as "America's First Planned Shopping Center." The center was executed by Chicago architect Howard Van Doren Shaw and included twenty-five stores, twelve offices and twenty-eight apartments in a 400- by 250-foot setting on Western Avenue. The design called for "rows or arcades in the eastern corners," and "two Tyrolean towers and an Italian Renaissance central building, across the west side, were all coordinated in cultivated taste and enduring beauty, making it one of the most attractive business centers in the country," wrote Lake Forest historian Edward Arpee in his book, *Lake Forest Illinois: History and Reminiscences 1861 -1961*. The center underwent a $1.5 million renovation in 2000 and is a historic fixture of the community.[170]

Park Forest Plaza (1949): Credited with being the first regional suburban shopping center in Chicagoland and one of the first, possibly even the second, in the nation. The planned community of Park Forest gained national attention when its construction was announced in 1946 on the heels of the Second World War. Its plan to provide affordable housing and services to returning combat veterans gave it the nickname of "GI Town." It gained further attention as the case study for William H. Whyte's famous treatise on suburban living, *The Organization Man*. In addition to a variety of housing options and plentiful parks, it featured a community shopping center based on the design of the Plaza San Marco in Venice.[171] The center was originally anchored by Sears, Goldblatt's and Marshall Field's, which contained a popular restaurant called the Trail Room. Like so many other early shopping centers, Park Forest Plaza was hurt by competition from larger, newer centers in the area, such as Lincoln and Orland Square Malls. The plaza was rebranded as the Centre of Park Forest in the late 1980s. As of October 2010, the now-vacated Marshall Field's was slated for demolition.[172] The village is now overseeing the conversion of the center to a mixed-use, traditional downtown. It is now known simply as DownTown Park Forest.[173]

EVERGREEN PLAZA (1952): Also one of Chicago's earliest suburban shopping centers, Evergreen Plaza was constructed by powerhouse Chicago developer Arthur Rubloff. It began as a combination of several stores anchored by two grocery stores in an open-air center. With the addition of new tenants, the mall was eventually fully enclosed. Now known simply as "The Plaza," it is still very much alive and well in south-suburban Evergreen Park at Ninety-fifth and Western Streets.[174]

HARLEM-IRVING PLAZA (1956): Located in Norridge Park, Harlem-Irving Plaza opened as a forty-five-store, open-air shopping center that included tenants such as Wieboldt's, Kroger, Fannie May, W.T. Grand, Woolworth's and Lerner's and was the eighty-ninth charter member of the International Council of Shopping Centers. In the 1960s, it was home to one of the first "Safety Towns." After the addition of anchors throughout the decades, and a multimillion-dollar facelift in 2004, it emerged from its fiftieth birthday in 2006 as a strong shopping center. As of 2010, it has cleverly rebranded itself as "HIP" and remains economically vibrant.[175]

OLD ORCHARD (1956): Old Orchard is an open-air shopping center in Skokie, Illinois, less than twenty miles east of Randhurst. Designed by Chicago retail standouts Loebl Schlossman & Hackl, the center was constructed to coordinate with the opening of the Edens Expressway. It was originally anchored at either end by The Fair and Montgomery Ward. Because all the tenants wanted to be near anchor Marshall Field's, the large department store was built in the middle of the center. The *Chicago Tribune* referred to Old Orchard at the time of Randhurst's construction as "the Crown Jewel of Chicago's suburban shopping center ring." Interestingly, with the exception of an addition of an enclosed food court, the mall has always embraced its open-air status. Various redevelopments have always shown an attention to landscaping. The mall remains a thriving member of Chicago's list of top shopping centers.[176] Though he was not involved in designing the center, Victor Gruen commented on its aesthetics in *The Heart of Our Cities* in 1962, stating, "I should like to mention Old Orchard, near Chicago for its especially beautiful treatment of landscaping and particularly for its tree-shaded parking area."[177]

GOLF MILL (1960): Golf Mill was constructed as an open-air shopping center in Niles, Illinois, and anchored by a large Sears store. Some of the features that set it apart from other centers were the live theater venue, Mill Run Theater, and the Millionaire Club, which was a reputed mob hangout. Despite the addition of other anchors, by the 1980s, Golf Mill was not keeping pace with nearby centers, such as Old Orchard, Randhurst and Woodfield, and was fully enclosed in 1985. Its most recent renovation occurred in 2006, and it remains open today as a viable mall. Observers of Golf Mill have credited its survival to its ability to serve a very important niche in the middle-class near-north and near-northwest suburbs of Chicago, offering an alternative to the posh malls located farther outside the city.[178]

OAKBROOK CENTER (1962): Located in west suburban Oak Brook, Illinois, very near Lombard's Yorktown Center, the shopping center is a remarkable success story, given its age. It was constructed in 1962 only four years after the Village of Oak Brook's incorporation and was initially occupied by Marshall Field & Company, Sears and C.D. Peacock. It now includes unapologetically upscale Bonwit Teller, Lord & Taylor, I. Magnin, Neiman-Marcus, Saks Fifth Avenue and numerous smaller specialty stores and chain shops. The center is said to have a parklike atmosphere and, in a move that would surely please Victor Gruen, hosts a number of community events, including summer concerts.[179] The company's website bills the center as "the largest open-air premier shopping center in the country...one of the most prestigious and striking outdoor shopping destinations in the Chicago area."[180] In a sentence, it would appear as though Oakbrook Center has successfully combined Woodfield's girth with Old Orchard's aesthetics.

DIXIE SQUARE (1965): Dixie Square is a mall that is perhaps most famous for its death. Constructed as a model shopping mall for the future, it grew to sixty-four stores by 1968. However, a staggering construction debt and high crime rate in Harvey, Illinois, led to its demise. As the *Chicagoist* correctly noted, "Of course, any discussion of Dixie Square Mall can't occur without bringing up one of the greatest car chase scenes of all time." This refers to the famous scene from the film *The Blues Brothers*, which was shot on location at the mall.[181] Dixie Square was essentially rebuilt to shoot this scene after it closed to the public in 1979. (Because of this, Dixie Square and Randhurst are kindred spirits, as the "Bluesmobile" used in the scene was a former Mount Prospect police cruiser). Amazingly, Dixie Square, though completely shuttered and deteriorating, remains standing to this day. It has been cited as the "worst-case" scenario of a dead mall and serves as a quintessential metaphor for the excesses of shopping center construction in the late 1960s and '70s, as well as racial disparities in the Chicago Southland. Plans are in the works for its demolition and redevelopment.

FORD CITY (1965): Something of an anomaly since this regional shopping center is located in Chicago proper, Ford City is situated at Cicero Avenue and Seventy-third Street in the West Lawn neighborhood. The area was originally developed during World War II as a plant that constructed B-29 bomber engines, when it was very much the outskirts of the city. It was later retrofitted for automobile production for Tucker Corporation and then Ford Motor Company. Once abandoned, developers cut into the building to separate a portion for a mall. The mall opened in 1965 as Ford City. The large building was separated into two halves—a strip mall and an enclosed mall. Sears anchors the strip mall portion, which is connected to the main building by a tunnel called "The Connection." It utilizes the basement between the severed halves of the buildings directly below the parking lot. The Connection used to be called Peacock Alley in the late '60s and early '70s, when it gained an unfortunate reputation for drug use and violence. Wieboldt's occupied the western-facing space until 1987, when Carson, Pirie, Scott & Co. moved in. The southern-facing space was last occupied by Montgomery Ward until that chain's bankruptcy. It is presently unoccupied. J.C. Penney occupies the eastern-facing space. Plans are in the works for Ford City's redevelopment, and it has been reported that the Chicago Transit Authority is considering extending its Orange Line train to the shopping center.[182]

YORKTOWN CENTER (1968): Yorktown Center was originally anchored by Randhurst Corporation partners Carson, Pirie, Scott & Co., Wieboldt's and Montgomery Ward, as well as J.C. Penney. Located in the western suburb of

Lombard, it was billed as the largest shopping center in the world when it was completed. It remains economically healthy and, as of 2010, continues to be anchored by J.C. Penney and Carson's, as well as Von Maur, which is the company's largest store. It is currently ringed by a large, upscale Westin Hotel that contains Chicago-favorite Harry Caray's Italian Steakhouse. In an interesting arrangement, the general merchandise sales tax rate for Yorktown Center stores is 9.25 percent, yet outside the Mall Ring Road, the sales tax rate for Lombard is 8.25 percent. Some of the store locations are required to charge higher rates than others, based on the address of the store.[183]

LAKEHURST MALL (1971): Located in Waukegan, Illinois, the mall was a joint venture of Carson, Pirie, Scott & Co. and Wieboldt's. In addition to its name and anchors, the mall had much in common with Randhurst. Its three anchors were Carson's, Wieboldt's and J.C. Penney. The mall was constructed with the anticipation of a fourth anchor, but this plan never materialized, and the space sat vacant throughout the life of the mall. One feature that made the mall prominent was the exterior of the Carson's store, which was lavishly decorated with salmon and cream-stripe motif, a radical departure from the normally conservative store architecture. The mall, seemingly doomed from the start by the absence of a fourth anchor, and further devastated by nearby Gurnee Mills, was demolished in 2004, after being "dead" for a number of years.[184]

WOODFIELD MALL (1972): To this day, Woodfield is a retail powerhouse, not only regionally, but also nationally. It is listed by the International Council of Shopping Centers as the fifth-largest shopping mall in the world and is one of Illinois' most visited sites. Its recent nearby Streets of Woodfield development is similar to Randhurst Village. The enclosed portion of the mall remains economically booming. In recent years, Woodfield grew so large that it was given a new designation, considered to be the first "super-regional" mall in America due to its ability to attract shoppers from far and wide.[185]

LINCOLN MALL (1973): One of the largest malls in Chicago's Southland at its opening, Lincoln Mall was located on Lincoln Highway and Cicero Avenue, just east of Interstate 57. When completed, it contained over one million square feet of space and had a strong alliance of anchor stores, including J.C. Penney, Wieboldt's, Sears and Montgomery Ward. It was very similar in design to its contemporaries, Lakehurst Mall and Yorktown Center. While it predated it by three years, Lincoln Mall was negatively affected by the construction and redevelopment of Orland Square Mall. Lincoln Mall was also weakened by the loss of anchor stores in the 1990s. As of 2010, it remains open but is widely considered to be a "dead mall."[186]

NORTHBROOK COURT (1976): Perhaps Chicago's most-filmed suburban shopping center, Northbrook was designed as an upscale mall anchored by Nieman Marcus, Sears, I. Magnin and Lord & Taylor. Sears closed in the 1980s and was replaced by J.C. Penney, while I. Magnin closed in 1992 and was demolished for the construction of a General Cinema multiplex theater. J.C. Penney, in turn, closed in 1992 and was razed; in its place was built Marshall Field's, which opened in 1995. The General Cinema was acquired by AMC Theatres in 2001, while outside the mall, a freestanding Crate & Barrel home furnishings store was opened in 2002. The mall, along with the community of Northbrook, has also been showcased around the world through various films. A scene from the 1980 Academy Award–winning *Ordinary People* was filmed on the escalators at Neiman Marcus, showing Mary Tyler Moore's character, Beth, in her public persona. The 1985 John Hughes film *Weird Science* also contained a scene shot at Northbrook Court.[187]

ORLAND SQUARE MALL (1976): Orland Square has been a successful fully enclosed mall since its inception, and little is noted about its history. It has enjoyed hegemony more than most malls and seen few changes over the years, likely due to the stability of its anchors, Sears, J.C. Penney, Macy's and Carson's. As a testament to just how many shopping centers were being built during this period, the smaller, enclosed Orland Park Place Mall was built across 151st Street, less than one mile south of Orland Park. It quickly became a dead mall, having an unfortunate lineup of anchors: Montgomery Ward, Wieboldt's and Main Street (now Kohl's).[188] Orland Park trustee Pat Gira went as far as to say that it was not only *a* dead mall but *the* dead mall: "This was known as the dead mall. Everyone knew the area by that name." The mall was completely demolished and replaced with an open-air, upscale promotional center in 1998. As of 2008, the redevelopment has had a positive economic impact.[189]

WATER TOWER PLACE (1976): Water Tower Place was known as the first "vertical" shopping center. Located in downtown Chicago on Michigan Avenue, the seven-story, 750,000-square-foot shopping center is credited with helping to give Michigan Avenue its reputation as Chicago's premier shopping street, replacing State Street (though State remains a very close second place). As one observer succinctly put it, "Nestled in the heart of downtown, and housing the flagship stores of Carson, Pirie, Scott and Marshall Field's, State Street retained its old-fashioned image of utility, while Michigan Avenue stole all the glitz and glamour." Water Tower Place remains a popular shopping center today, with popular stores such as American Girl and the Drury Lane Theater. It is accompanied by several other vertical shopping malls in downtown Chicago, including State Street redevelopment Block 37, the Atrium Mall in the James R. Thompson Center, Shops at the Mart at the massive Art Deco Merchandise Mart Building, the Shops at Northbridge, (the dying) Chicago Place and 900 North Michigan Shops, the tallest building in the United States to house a shopping mall.[190]

GURNEE MILLS (1991): One of the first "outlet malls" to come to Chicago, Gurnee Mills was constructed in 1991 in Gurnee, Illinois, also home to Six Flags Great America theme park. The center was also located seven miles from Lakehurst Mall, but its developers asserted, incorrectly, that the mall would not harm Lakehurst because it focused on outlet, as opposed to retail, shopping. This would not prove to be the case, and while Lakehurst has disappeared, Gurnee Mills continues to be a Chicago shopping destination.[191]

DEER PARK TOWN CENTER (2000): A newcomer to the suburban Chicago shopping centers, Deer Park was among the first outdoor "lifestyle centers," which are characterized by upscale retailers with ample and easy parking—or, as one developer called them, "malls without halls." Deer Park, located not far from Randhurst on Rand Road, along with Woodfield, was accused of contributing to Randhurst's demise. It is interesting to note, however, that the concepts for Randhurst Village borrow heavily from Deer Park.

Appendix B
Randhurst Directories

1962

Carson, Pirie, Scott & Co.
The Fair–Randhurst
Wieboldt's
Almer Coe Optical Company
Apple Basket Restaurant
Baker's Shoe Store
Baskin
Benson-Rixon
Brautigam Florist-Gifts
Carson, Pirie, Scott &
  Co. Restaurants
    The Tree Top Restaurant
    The Bird's Nest Cocktail Lounge
    Pancake Shop
    Tartan Tray Cafeteria
Chandler's Shoe Store
Claire Hats
Cover Girl
Craft Studio
Dutch Mill Candies
Emery's Tailor Shop
Fabric Mart
Flagg Brothers Store
The Florsheim Shoe Shop
Frank Jewelers
Hosiery Bar
Jewel Food Store
Karpet Show Case
Kay Campbell's
Kinny Shoes
Kresge's
Lauter's
La Petit Café
Le Rendezvous Snack Bar
William A. Lewis
Lorsey's Fashion Accessories
Marianne Shops
Norman's
O'Connor & Goldberg Shoes
Randhurst Bank
Randhurst Barbershop
Randhurst Camera Shop

Randhurst Corned Beef Center
Randhurst Heel Bar
Randhurst Key Shop
Randhurst Music Center
Randhurst Tie Rack
Maurice L. Rothschild
Singer Sewing Center of Randhurst
Stivers Office Service (Professional Level)
Stuart's
Sun Self-Serv Drugs
Tedd's Sportswear
Walton Rug & Furniture Co.
Youthful Shoes

CIRCA 1965

Carson, Pirie, Scott & Co.
Montgomery Ward–Randhurst
Wieboldt's
Almer Coe Optical Company
The Americana Shop
Apple Basket Restaurant
Bak Photo Studio
Baker's Shoe Store
Baskin
Beau Monde Boutique
Benson-Rixon
Bombay Shop
Brautigam Florist-Gifts
Candle Shop
Carson's International Restaurants
  The Tree Top Restaurant
  The Bird's Nest Cocktail Lounge
  Tartan Tray Cafeteria
Chandler's Shoe Store
Claire Hats
Cover Girl
Dutch Mill Candies
Emery's Tailor Shop
Fabric Mart
Famous Beauty Salon
First National Bank
Flagg Brothers Shoes
The Florsheim Shoe Shop
Frank Jewelers
Frannz Creative Corner
Gangi Continental Shop
Garfield's Gift Shop
Hickory Farms
Jewel Food Store
Kay Campbell's
Kinney Shoes
Knit & Purl
Kresge's
Kushen Bros. Furniture
Lane Bryant
Lauter's Men's Wear
La Petit Café
Le Rendezvous Snack Bar
William A. Lewis
Lorsey's Fashion Accessories
Lyon-Healy
Marianne Shop
Normans
O'Connor & Goldberg Shoes
Pam's Children's Wear
Paradise Tours
Parklane Hosiery
Randhurst Art Gallery
Randhurst Barbershop
Randhurst Camera Shop
Randhurst Corned Beef Center
Randhurst Heel Bar
Randhurst Key Shop
Randhurst Music Center
Randhurst Shaver Shop

Randhurst Tie Rack
Randhurst Toy Kiosk
June Rold Dance Studio
Maurice L. Rothschild
Seno & Sons
Singer Sewing Center
Sporting Goods Shop
Stuart's
Sun Self-Serv Drugs
Tedd's Sportswear
Walton Rug & Furniture Co.
White Collar Girls of America
Youthful Shoes

Professional Offices–Upper Level

Georgiann Chapman, RN,
 Electrolysis
French Cafés, Inc.
Sidney D. Gault, DDS
General Electric Credit Corp.
Frank E. Grogman, DDS
Manufacturers Life Insurance Co.
Dwaine F. Marquette, DDS
Mr. Minimum, Inc.
National Insurers Service Co.
Robert E. Penn, MD,
 Ophthalmologist
Prospect Clinical Laboratory
Randhurst Accounting & Data
 Processing Service
Safeco Insurance Group of
 America
S.S. Kresge Co.
Stivers Office Service
Traveler's Insurance Co.
Robert E. Vraney, DDS
James R. Waldman, DDS

Circa 1970

Carson, Pirie, Scott & Co.
Montgomery Ward–Randhurst
Wieboldt's
Almer Coe Optical Company
The Americana Shop
Bak Photo Studio
Baker's Shoe Store
Baskin Clothing Company
Beau Monde Boutique
Benson-Rixon
Bombay Shop
Brautigam Florist-Gifts
Candle Nook
Carson's International Restaurants
 The Tree Top Restaurant
 The Bird's Nest Cocktail Lounge
 Tartan Tray Cafeteria
Chandler's Shoe Store
Claire's Boutique
Cover Girl
Dolores Eiler School of Dance
Dutch Mill Candies
Emery's Tailor Shop
Fabric Mart
Fell-Rudman & Co.
First National Bank
Flagg Brothers Shoes
The Florsheim Shoe Shop
Frank Jewelers
Frannz Party & Gag Shop
Gangi Continental Shop
Garfield's Gift Studio
Hickory Farms
Kay Campbell's
Kinney Shoes
Knit & Purl
Kresge's

Kushen Bros. Furniture
Lane Bryant
Lauter's Men's Wear
La Petit Café
Left Bank Book Shop & Art Supplies
Le Rendezvous Snack Bar
Mary Lester Fabrics
William A. Lewis
Lorsey's Fashion Accessories
Lyon-Healy
Marianne Shop
Mid-America Research
Normans
O'Connor & Goldberg Shoes
On Stage
Pam's Children's Wear
Paradise Tours
Parklane Hosiery
Randee's Restaurant
Randhurst Art Gallery
Randhurst Barbershop
Randhurst Camera Shop
Randhurst Corned Beef Center
Randhurst Key Shop
Randhurst Music Center
Randhurst Shaver Shop
Randhurst Tie Rack
Randhurst Toy Kiosk
June Rold Dance Studio
Maurice L. Rothschild
Seno & Sons
Shoe Repair
Singer Sewing Center
Sporting Goods Shop
Chas. A. Stevens
Stuart's
Sun Self-Serv Drugs
Tedd's Sportswear
Toys by Rizzi
Trident Office Supplies
Walton Rug & Furniture Co.
White Collar Girls of America
Youthful Shoes

Professional Offices–Upper Level

H.R. Bruhl Accounting & Income Tax
Chapman Electrolysis, Georgiann Chapman, RN
Costello & Trumfio, DDS
Donovan & Assoc. RW, Orthodontist
Dr. Harold Feinhandler, Ophthalmologist
French Cafes, Inc.
General Electric Co.
General Electric Credit Corp.
General Insurance Company of America
Grogman, Frank E., DDS
Holmes & Associates
Illinois Counties Patrol
Kresge Company
Dwain F. Marquette, DDS
The Singer Co.
Stivers Lifesavers, Inc.
Traveler's Insurance Company
James R Waldman., DDS

1977

Carson, Pirie, Scott & Co.
Montgomery Ward–Randhurst
Wieboldt's
The Americana Shop
Baker's Shoe Store
Barbara's

Baskin
Bath & A-Half
Brautigam's Florist
Brautigam's Mini-Mart
Candle Nook
Card Shop
Chandler's Shoe Store
Chicago Organ and Piano
Claire's Boutique
Cover Girl
Craft Corner
Cutlery World
Delores Eiler Dance Studio
Different Circle
Fanny Farmer Candies
First National Bank of Mount Prospect
Flagg Bros. Shoes
Florsheim Shoes
Foot Locker
Frank Jewelers
Garfield's Gift Studio
General Nutrition Center
Hickory Farms
Hot Sam
House of Lewis
House of Photography
House of Vision
I-Beam Shop
Jeans West
Just Pants
Karoll's Men's Fashions
Kay Campbell
Kinney Shoes
Kresge
Kroch & Brentano's
L'Elegance
Lane Bryant
Leather, etc.
Lerner's
William A. Lewis
Lorsey's Fashion Accessories
Lyon-Healy
Marianne Shop
Meat 'N' Place
Merle Norman
Money Store
O'Connor & Goldberg Shoes
On Stage
Pam's Children's Wear
Paradise Tours
Parklane Hosiery
Patisserie Bakery & Coffeehouse
Pet World
Picture Perfect Frame Shop
P.J.'s Trick Shop
Randee's
Randhurst Barbershop
Randhurst Engraving World
Randhurst Key Shop
Randhurst Music Center
Randhurst Photo
Randhurst Shoe Repair
Randhurst Wallpaper & Paint Shop
The Reunion
Maurice L. Rothschild
Ryan's Coins and Stamps
Seno & Sons
Shaver's World
Shirts Only
Singer Sewing Center
Sports Chalet
Chas. A. Stevens
Stuart's
Susie's Casuals
Tailor Shop
Tartan Tray Cafeteria
Tedd's Teepee

Toys by Rizzi
Youthful Shoes

Professional Offices–Upper Level

Accountants Temporary Personnel
American Society of Mechanical Engineers
William B. Brand, Optometrist
H.R. Bruhl, Data Processing
Casey Services, Inc.
Chapman Electrolysis
Costello, Trumfio & Mategrano, DDS
Creative Advertising Service
Elema-Schonander, Inc.
GECC Financial Services
General Electric Credit Corp.
German American National Congress
M.E. Hunter, Tax Offices, Inc
Illinois Counties Detective & Patrol Agency
Illinois Fire Inspectors Assoc.
John Lehrer Associates
Mid America Research
S&C Insurance
State Farm Insurance
Stivers Temporary Personnel
James R. Waldman, DDS
West Personnel
White Collar Girls

Free Standing Stores and Services

Monterey Whaling Village–Rand & Elmhurst
Child World–Foundry
Ward's Auto Center–Foundry
Bell Federal Savings & Loan–Foundry
CARS Auto Service–Euclid
Randhurst Cinema–Euclid
Jewel/Osco–Euclid
Recycling Center

CIRCA 1983

Carson, Pirie, Scott & Co.
Montgomery Ward
Wieboldt's
Americana Shop
Baker's Shoe Store
Barbara's
Baskin
Bath & A-Half
Benson's House of Vision
Brautigam's Florist
CPI Photo Finish
Camelot Music
Career Image
Caren Charles
Chandler's Shoes
Chez Chocolate
Claire's Boutique
Coffee Bean
The Confectionary
Cover Girl
Craft Corner
Cutlery World
Emporium Luggage
Fanny Farmer Candies
First National Bank of Mount Prospect
Flagg Bros. Shoes
Florsheim Shoes
Foot Locker

Frank Jewelers
General Nutrition Center
Gingiss Formalwear
Hickory Farms
Hush Puppies Shoes
Jeans West
Jewel Box
Joann Fabrics/Singer
Just Pants
Karoll's Men's Fashions
Kay Campbell
Kinney Shoes
Kroch & Brentano's
L'Elegance
Lane Bryant
Leather, Etc.
Lerner's
Merle Norman
Music Box Etc.
Naturalizer Shoes
Noah's Ark
O'Connor & Goldberg Shoes
O'Neill's Card Shop
Open Country
Original Cookie Company
P.J.'s Trick Shop
Pam's Children's Wear
Paradise Tours
Parklane Hosiery
Patisserie Bakery & Coffeehouse
Picture Perfect Frame Shop
Potpourri
Prints Plus
Radio Shack
Randee's Restaurant
Randhurst Engraving World
Randhurst Hair Designs
Randhurst Key Shop
Randhurst Music Center
Randhurst Photo
Randhurst Shoe Repair
Randhurst Tailor Shop
Red Cross Shoes
Regis Hairstyles
Reuss' Sports & Ski
Reunion
Maurice L. Rothschild
Ryan's Coins and Stamps
Shaver's World
Splendiferous
Chas A. Stevens
Stride Rite
Stuart's
Sunshine Cottage
Supercade
Susie's Casuals
Tedd's
This End Up
Tickled Pink Maternity
Toys by Rizzi
Ups 'N' Downs
Woman's World

Professional Offices–Upper Level

American Society of Mechanical Engineers
Analytics, Inc.
Patrick J. Angelo, DDS, MS, Periodontist
Chapman Electrolysis
Costello, Trumfio & Mategrano, DDS
Gottschalk Claim Service
Mid America Research
Money Store
James R. Waldman, DDS

Concourse Level

Counseling Services Associates
German American National Congress
M.E. Hunter, Tax Offices, Inc.
Sandra Kay Associates, Inc.
John Lehrer Associates, Inc.
Randhurst Babysitting Center
Randhurst Obstetrics & Gynecology, SC
Denise Sabala Dance Studio
State Farm Insurance
Stivers Temporary Personnel
White Collar Services, Ltd.

Circa 1995

Gifts, Books and Stationery

Americana Shop
Brautigam's Florist
Kroch's & Brentano's
Lemstone Books
Names Plus
The Nature of Things Store
O'Neill's Hallmark
Potpourri
Things Remembered
With Best Wishes
The Wooden Bird

Children's Apparel, Shoes and Toys

KayBee Toys
Lady Foot Locker
Payless Shoe Source
Stride-Rite

Department Stores

Carson, Pirie, Scott & Co.
Carson, Pirie, Scott & Co. Home Furnishings
Filene's Basement
J.C. Penney
Kohl's
Montgomery Ward

Women's Fashions

Au Coton
August Max Woman
Barrie Pace, Ltd. for Baskin
Benetton
Caren Charles
Casual Corner
County Seat
Lerner
Limited
Limited Express
Merry-Go-Round
Motherhood Maternity
Northern Reflections
Petite Sophisticate
Rave
Stuart's
Ups 'N' Downs
Wilson's Suede & Leather
Woman's World

Men's Fashion

Bachrach
Baskin
Club International
County Seat
Gingiss Formalwear

J. Riggings
J.W.
Merry-Go-Round
Wilson's Suede & Leather

Jewelry & Accessories

Accessory Lady
Afterthoughts
Barbara's Jewelers
Claire's Boutique
Frank Jewelers
Lundstrom Jewelers
Rolland's Jewelers
Sunsations Sunglass Company
Zales

Shoes

The Athlete's Foot
Baker's Shoes
Castleby
Cobbie Shop
Florsheim
Foot Locker
Hush Puppies
Kinney
Lady Foot Locker
Naturalizer
Nine West
Payless Shoe Source

Records, Tapes, Electronics and Computer

Camelot Music
Radio Shack
Software, Etc.
Tape World

Home Furnishings

Bombay Company
Burress Furniture
The Country Bin
Deck the Walls
Lady Jane
Lechters Housewares
This End Up
Young Kil Oriental Imports

Health and Beauty Services

The Body Shop
Fantasy Faces
General Nutrition Center
Merle Norman Cosmetics
Randhurst Hair Design
Regis Hairstyles
Service Optical
Trade Secret

Specialty Stores

Beer Stuff
Blarney
Brautigam's Florist
Cutlery World/Shaver's World
Emporium Luggage
Garden of Bead'n
Monograms USA
Moondog's Comicland
Party Zone
Ritz Camera & One Hour Photo
Ryan's Coins, Jewelry & Baseball Cards
Sir Richard of Randhurst
Sunshine Cottage

Sporting Goods and Apparel

The Athlete's Foot
Champs
Foot Locker
Lady Foot Locker
Team Spirit

The Picnic

A&W Hot Dogs
Bain's Deli
Boardwalk Fries
Bon Appetit
Charley's Steakery
Dunkin' Donuts
Everything Yogurt
Hot Sam
The Ice Cream Club
Manchu Wok
McDonald's
One Potato Two
Sakkio Japan
Sbarro's Pizza

Specialty Food

Coffee Depot
Door County Confectionary
Fannie May
Michael's Bakery & Café
Original Cookie Co.
Tropik Sun, Fruit & Nut

Restaurants

Applebee's (Coming Soon)

Services

Bell Federal Savings
Brautigam's Florist
Customer Service Center
Illinois Job Service
NBD Bank of Mount Prospect
Paradise Travel
Party Zone
Randhurst Tailor
Ritz Camera & One Hour Photo
Sears Portrait Studio
Things Remembered
Ticketmaster (Carson Pirie Scott)
U.S. Post Office Shipping Station

Drug, Variety and Supermarket

Bataille Academie of Dance
Costello, Trumfio & Montegrano
E.H. Schmitz Realty
Everything's $1
Jewel/Osco
Khipple, Dr. S., MD
Market Shares Corporation
M.E. Hunter Tax Service
Mid-America Research
Rolland's Corporate Office
State Farm Insurance
Waldman, James, DDS
Woolworth Express

CIRCA 2000

Department Stores

Carson, Pirie, Scott & Co.
Circuit City

Home Depot
J.C. Penney
Kohl's
Montgomery Ward
Old Navy Clothing Co.

Women's Apparel and Accessories

Afterthoughts
August Max Woman
Casual Corner
Claire's Boutique
Coopers Watchworld
County Seat
Express
Frederick's of Hollywood
Hot Rags
Leather Image
Lerner New York
Limited
Modern Woman
Motherhood Maternity
Northern Reflections
Paul Harris
Petite Sophisticate
Rave
Sunglass Hut
Victoria's Secret
Wilson's Suede & Leather

Men's Apparel and Accessories

Coopers Watchworld
County Seat
Gingiss Formalwear
Leather Image
New York City
Sunglass Hut
Wilson's Suede & Leather

Children's Apparel, Books and Toys

Children's Place
Comix Revolution
Kaybee Toys
Lemstone Books
Waldenbooks
World of Science

Shoes

Athlete's Foot
Champs Sports
Easy Spirit
Florsheim Shoes
Foot Locker
Hush Puppies
Kinney Shoes
Lady Foot Locker
Naturalizer
Nine West
Payless Shoe Source
Stride Rite

Books and Cards

Carlton Cards
Comix Revolution
Lemstone Books
O'Neill's Hallmark
Waldenbooks
With Best Wishes

Sporting Goods and Apparel

Athlete's Foot
Champs Sports
Chicago Sports Gifts
Foot Locker

Lady Foot Locker
Ryan's Coins, Jewelry & Baseball Cards

Jewelry

Barbara's Jewelers
Doerner Jewelers
Fast Fix Jewelry Repair
Lundstrom Jewelers
Noor's Jewelers
Piercing Pagoda
Ultra Jewelers
Zales

Health, Beauty and Haircare

Barrington Bath Shoppe
Bath & Body Works
The Body Shop
General Nutrition Center
Great Clips for Hair
Lovely Nails
Merle Norman Cosmetics
Regis Hairstyles
Trade Secret

Home Furnishings

The Bombay Company
Carson, Pirie, Scott Home Furnishings
Deck The Walls
Lechters Housewares
The Wooden Bird

Gifts and Luggage

Beer Stuff
Blarney Irish Gifts
Carlton Cards
Chicago Sports Gifts
Emporium Luggage
Lemstone Books
Monograms USA
O'Neill's Hallmark
Potpourri
Ritz Camera & One Hour Photo
Spencer Gifts
Suncoast Motion Picture Company
Sunshine Cottage
Things Remembered
With Best Wishes
The Wooden Bird
World of Science

Entertainment and Electronics

General Cinema
Music Recyclery
Radio Shack
Suncoast Motion Picture Company
Tape World
Ultra Zone

Services

Bell Federal Savings
Customer Service Center
Doc's Eyeglasses, Contacts, 1-Hour Lab
First Chicago Bank
Montgomery Ward Auto Express
Paradise Travel
Randhurst Shoe Repair
Randhurst Tailor
Ritz Camera & One Hour Photo
Sears Portrait Studio
U.S. Post Office Substation
Ticketmaster (Carson Pirie Scott)

Village of Mount Prospect
Resource Center

Food Court

A&W Hot Dogs
Baskin Robbins
Boardwalk Fries
Cajun & Grill
Charley's Steakery
McDonald's
Panda Express Chinese
Patisserie Too
Quencher Smoothies
Sakkio Japan
Sbarro's Italian Eatery
Subway

Restaurants

Applebee's
East Side Mario's
Hacienda

Specialty Food

Coffee Depot
Cinnabon
Door County Confectionary
Fannie May
Original Cookie Co.
Pretzelmaker

Drug, Variety and Supermarket

Dollar Tree
Jewel/Osco
Gateway Newstand

Professional Offices

Bataille Academie of Dance
Concept to Print, Inc.
Costello, Trumfio & Mategrano, DDS
Dolphin Mortgage
E.H. Schmintz Realty
Market Shares Corporation
Dr. H. Mavi, MD
M.E. Hunter Tax Service
Mid-America Research
Edward D. Jones & Co.
Dr. S. Khipple, MD
Dr. S. Orenstein, MD
State Farm Insurance
Waldman, James, DDS

Notes

Introduction

1. "Carson's Expert Tells Center Plans," *Mount Prospect Herald*, October 9, 1958.

Chapter 1

2. Early information on the history of Mount Prospect taken from Jean Murphy and Mary Wajer, *Mount Prospect: Where Town and Country Meet* (N.p., 1991).
3. Map of Busse & Wille's ReSubdivision, circa 1910, Mount Prospect Historical Society Collection.
4. Frederick Law Olmsted, papers from the planning of Riverside, Illinois, reprinted in *Landscape Architecture* (July 1931): 256–77, 280–87, 290–91.
5. Casmir Banas, "Shoppers' 'Paradise' Planned for Mt. Prospect," *Chicago Sunday Tribune*, July 17, 1960.

Chapter 2

6. "Helicopter Survey Clinches 80-Acre Carson Project," *Herald American*, August 21, 1958.

7. Chicago History Museum, *Encyclopedia of Chicago* online resource, "History of Carson Pirie Scott," http://www.encyclopedia.chicagohistory.org/pages/2586.html. This entry is part of the encyclopedia's *Dictionary of Leading Chicago Businesses* (1820–2000), prepared by Mark R. Wilson, with additional contributions from Stephen R. Porter and Janice L. Reiff.
8. "Carson Executive To Direct Project," *Mount Prospect Herald*, September 18, 1958.
9. Minutes of the Mount Prospect Zoning Commission, Tuesday, May 24, 1955, MPHS Randhurst Archives.
10. "History of The Fair," Pleasant Family Shopping online retail history resource, http://pleasantfamilyshopping.blogspot.com/2010/07/fair-comes-to-wards.html.
11. "Ward (Montgomery) & Co," *Encyclopedia of Chicago*, Chicago History Museum, http://www.encyclopedia.chicagohistory.org/pages/2895.html.
12. "FDR Seizes Control of Montgomery Ward," History.com, http://www.history.com/this-day-in-history/fdr-seizes-control-of-montgomery-ward.
13. "Wieboldt Stores, Inc.," *Encyclopedia of Chicago*, Chicago History Museum, http://encyclopedia.chicagohistory.org/pages/2903.html.
14. "Forgotten Chicago" online forum, http://www.forgottenchicago.com/forum/1/2622.
15. Dave Pauly, "3-Way Competition at Suburb Center," *Chicago Daily News*, July 25, 1962.
16. Ibid.
17. "Three Loop Stores To Promote Center: Carson's Announce Contract," *Mount Prospect Herald*, February 26, 1959.
18. Robert Ferguson and June Wille Wittmeyer, Oral History Files, Mount Prospect Historical Society.
19. Andy Logan and Brendan Gill, "The Talk of the Town," *New Yorker*, March 17, 1956.

CHAPTER 3

20. While proper citations have been included, the vast majority of research in this chapter comes almost verbatim from M. Jeffrey Hardwick's *Mall Maker: Victor Gruen, Architect of an American Dream* (Philadelphia: University of Pennsylvania Press, 2004). I neither have the will nor the eloquence to attempt to rewrite Mr. Hardwick's definitive biography. I am merely attempting to portray Gruen in the specific context of Randhurst, though by doing so,

wider implications to Gruen's early life and body of work—and as a result, Hardwick's work—are made. I am indebted to the latter for the use of his research and his personal assistance in this work and would recommend that any serious-minded student of history, especially architectural and retail history, refer to his book.

21. Early biographical information as quoted in Hardwick, *Mall Maker*, 9–11.
22. Hardwick, *Mall Maker*, 12–13.
23. As quoted in Hardwick, *Mall Maker*, 1.
24. "Refugees Who Made a Difference: Victor Gruen," United Nations High Commissioner on Refugees, http://www.unhcr.org/pages/49c3646c74-page6.html.
25. Hardwick, *Mall Maker*, 13–15.
26. As quoted in Hardwick, *Mall Maker*, 15.
27. Ibid.
28. Ibid., 22–23.
29. Ibid., 23.
30. Ibid., 101.
31. Ibid., 104.
32. Ibid., 104.
33. "Cities: Footpaths in Fort Worth," *Time*, March 19, 1956.
34. Ibid.
35. As quoted in Hardwick, *Mall Maker*, 151.
36. Tony Wietzel, Unknown Newspaper, August 21, 1962.
37. See http://www.abc.net.au/tv/gruentransfer/faq.htm. The Gruen Transfer is also discussed in detail in Hardwick, *Mall Maker*, 1–3, and in various articles and blogs.
38. "Huge Randhurst Center Project Opened," *Chicago Daily Construction News*, August 31, 1962.

Chapter 4

39. "Randhurst Promotes G.M. O'Neill," *Chicago Daily News*, August 8, 1962.
40. *Chicago Daily News*, November 18, 1960. Photo by Edmund Jarecki.
41. "'Hot' Promotion for Shopping Center," *Mount Prospect Herald*, November 24, 1960.
42. "Carlos Diniz Biography," Edward Cella Art and Architecture, http://www.edwardcella.com/html/ArtistBio.asp?artist=81.

43. "Largest Center Under One Roof Saves Steps with Multi-Level Design," Otis Elevator Company Public Relations Press Release, October 24, 1961.
44. As quoted in Dave Aldrich, "Requiem For Randhurst," Pleasant Family Shopping, http://pleasantfamilyshopping.blogspot.com/2008/10/requiem-for-randhurst.html.
45. Press release from Herbert M. Kraus & Co. for Victor Gruen Associates, May 13, 1960. Mount Prospect Historical Society, 1996.
46. "Randhurst Water Tower…New Landmark for These Suburbs," *Arlington Heights Herald*, July 5, 1962.
47. "Randhurst Makes $6,000 Payment," *Mount Prospect Herald*, November 10, 1960.
48. John Slania, "Randhurst Mall Still Shines on Silver Anniversary," *Daily Herald*, September 13, 1987.
49. Randi Hurst, "Randhurst Memories," Unknown Publication, September 10, 1987.
50. "Randhurst Center Celebrates Via 'Domestone' Laying Rights," *Paddock Publications*, March 8, 1962.
51. "Randhurst at Another Milestone," *Mount Prospect Herald*, March 8, 1962.
52. "Mayor Schlaver Speaks at Randhurst Domestone Ceremony," *Mount Prospect Independent*, March 8, 1962.
53. Melda Lynn, "First Woman Visitor Reports on Growth at Randhurst," *Mount Prospect Herald*, August 10, 1961.
54. Melda Lynn, "Meet Women Behind Mammoth Randhurst," *Mount Prospect Herald*, March 22, 1962.
55. "Workman at Randhurst Falls 2 Stories; Condition 'Fair,'" *Arlington Heights Herald*, February 1, 1962.
56. "Roofer Dies of Injury in Fall Off Scaffold," *Sunday Sun-Times*, July 1, 1962.

CHAPTER 5

57. George M. O'Neill and Randhurst Corporation's Letter to Mount Prospect Residents, July 28, 1962 (MPHS Randhurst Archives–1994.20.90 Ltr to 400 S. I-Oka C.O. Schlaver).
58. "50-Page Section on Center Sets Tribune Record," *Chicago Daily Tribune*, n.d.
59. "Welfare Unit will Preview Shopping Center," *Chicago Daily Tribune*, August 9, 1962.

60. Melda Lynn, "Lavish Dinner-Dance Benefit Fete Is 'Sneak Preview,'" *Cook County Herald*, August 16, 1962.
61. "Randhurst Gets Finishing Touches," Unknown Newspaper, August 14, 1962.
62. Hal Foust, "Finish Major Road of Junior Expressway," *Chicago Daily Tribune*, August 15, 1962.
63. "Randhurst Donates Funds for Roadway," *Mount Prospect Herald*, June 7, 1962.
64. "Fast Rail, Bus Service Begun to Randhurst," *Chicago's American*, August 20, 1962.
65. "Little Girl Cuts Ribbon to Start Things Rolling at Randhurst," *Chicago's American*, August 16, 1962.
66. Randi Hurst, "Randhurst Memories," Unknown Publication, September 10, 1987, MPHS Randhurst Archives.
67. *The Randhurster*, October 1962, MPHS Randhurst Archives.
68. "Randhurst Offers Locker Convenience," *Chicago Daily Tribune*, August 16, 1962.
69. *Welcome to Randhurst*, Company Brochure, MPHS Randhurst Archives.
70. "Satisfy Shopper's Taste Under Randhurst Roof," *Chicago Daily Tribune*, August 16, 1962.
71. "New Wieboldt Store at Randhurst Has Prints of Our Youth," [Des Plaines] *Suburban Times*, August 9, 1962. (The fate of the handprints is unknown.)
72. Peg Zwecker, "Students' Mural Big Hit With Stores," *Chicago Daily News*, Friday, May 25, 1962.
73. Melda Lynn, "Pupils' Work Is Exhibited," *Arlington Heights Herald*, April 26, 1962.
74. Ibid.
75. "Famous U.S. Sculptors Exhibit Works at Center," *Chicago Daily Tribune*, August 16, 1962, MPHS Collection.
76. Ibid.
77. Randhurst Center Company Prospectus, "Presenting A New Dimension In Retailing," March 1, 1962, MPHS Randhurst Archives.
78. "Randhurst Jackpot' Hit By Local Woman," Unknown Publication, September 12, 1962, MPHS Randhurst Archives.
79. "Manager Answers Questions: How Will Randhurst Affect Communities?" *Paddock Publications*, November 24, 1960.
80. Special Advertising Section, *Chicago Tribune*, August 12, 1962.
81. http://www.chicagobauhausbeyond.org/cbb/mission/erickson.htm (accesssed August 25, 2010).

82. "All Freight to Randhurst Delivered via Giant Underground Tunnel," *Chicago Daily Tribune*, August 15, 1962.
83. Melda Lynn, "Little Bit of Florida Being Transplanted to Randhurst," *Mount Prospect Herald*, July 12, 1962.
84. "Huge Randhurst Center Project Opened," *Chicago Daily Construction News*, Friday, August 31, 1962.
85. "The Way We See It: Giant Randhurst Is A Welcome Addition," *Arlington Heights Herald*, August 16, 1962.

CHAPTER 6

86. *The Randhurster*, October 1962.
87. "North Cook 4-H Fair to Host Barn Dance," *Mount Prospect Herald*, Thursday, August 16, 1962.
88. Ibid.
89. "Auto Show at Randhurst," *Chicago Daily Tribune*, October 9, 1962.
90. "O'Neill Points Out Randhurst's Popcorn Concession Success," *Prospect Heights Herald*, September 27, 1962.
91. For more information regarding Ford City, see Appendix A.
92. Karen Lucas, "Mt. Prospect Services Grow As Sales Jump," *Chicago Tribune*, July 4, 1963.
93. "Randhurst Reporter," January 10, 1963, MPHS Randhurst Archives.
94. "Randhurst Memories," *Daily Herald*, September 24, 1987, Mount Prospect Public Library, Local History File.
95. "Randhurst Sales Hit Record During 1967," *Prospect Day*, February 14, 1968.

CHAPTER 7

96. "Meet the 'New America,'" *Chicago Tribune*, February 4, 1973.
97. "Woodfield Center Sets Ceremony," *Chicago Tribune*, October 9, 1969.
98. "Woodfield Mall Opening Set," *Chicago Tribune*, September 9, 1971.
99. "Woodfield Mall to Host Biggest Stores," *Chicago Tribune*, May 24, 1970.
100. Gerald West and Ronald Yates, "Work Still Goes On as Woodfield Opens," *Chicago Tribune*, September 10, 1971.
101. History of Schaumburg Township (HOST), http://ourlocalhistory.wordpress.com/2010/07/04/woodfield-mall-opening-day.

102. "Meet the 'New America.'"
103. William Sluis, "Woodfield Mall Hits Paydirt; Neighboring Suburbs Feel Bite," *Chicago Tribune*, May 25, 1972; ProQuest Historical Newspapers, *Chicago Tribune* (1849–1987).
104. "Meet the 'New America.'"
105. Ibid.
106. Ibid.
107. Fishman, *Bourgeois Utopias*, 184.
108. "Shopping Centers Are Also Doing Well," *Chicago Tribune*, Noember 7, 1971.
109. "Randhurst Center to Mark 9th Anniversary," *Chicago Tribune*, July 29, 1971.
110. "Randhurst Corp., Village Back In Bus Business," *Mount Prospect Herald*, March 20, 1972.
111. "Shoppers' Special Will Make Last Run June 17," *Mount Prospect Herald*, June 1, 1972.
112. "Hockey Arena Will Be Built at Randhurst," April 2, 1972.
113. "$1.5 Million Sport Center Slated For Randhurst," *Mount Prospect Herald*, March 29, 1972.
114. Bob Verdi, "Magnuson Rejoins Hawks against Sabres Tomorrow," October 23, 1973.
115. Bob Verdi, "Cardinal Icers Get Czech-Up Tomorrow," January 1, 1974. Further information regarding the Cardinals and the North American Hockey League was unavailable.
116. Jim Fitzgerald, "'74 Silver Skates to Be Held in New Arena," February 18, 1974.
117. Jim Fitzgerald, "Olympic Prospects Skate at Randhurst," March 16, 1974.
118. "Chicago Cougars," WHA Hockey, www.whahockey.com/cougars.html.
119. Ibid.
120. Ibid.
121. Ibid.
122. Art Dunn, "Randhurst Cougars vs. Toros tonight," *Chicago Tribune*, April 19, 1974.
123. David Condon, "Those Crazy Cougars Are Way Out Now," *In the Wake of the News*, April 26, 1974.
124. Bob Verdi, "4th Around the Corner—Hockey Awards Are Due," April 30, 1974.
125. Art Dunn, "Cougars vs. Toros Here Again," *Chicago Tribune*, April 30, 1974.

126. Ward Melanger, "Sound Off, Sports Fans!: New Football League Has a Bitter Enemy," May 1, 1974.

127. Art Dunn, "If Cougars Do Beat Toros…Then What?" *Chicago Tribune*, May 3, 1974.

128. Art Dunn, "Cougars Seek Equalizer," *Chicago Tribune*, May 4, 1974.

129. "If Cougars Do Beat Toros."

130. Art Dunn, "Cougars to Open WHA Finals Sunday in Randhurst," *Chicago Tribune*, May 8, 1974.

131. Evan Weiner, "Gordie's Favorite Feat: Playing Hockey with Sons," NHL.com, http://www.nhl.com/ice/news.htm?id=522876, accessed August 11, 2010.

132. *Herald*, September 4, 1972.

133. Mary Anne Hannemann, "New Look Marks Randhurst's 15th Year," Unknown newspaper, Mount Prospect Public Library Local History File.

134. George Lazarus, "Woodfield Keeps Top Shopping Center Spot," *Chicago Tribune*, March 11, 1979.

135. Robert Davis, "Roofs in Peril: Buildings Closed," *Chicago Tribune*, January 27, 1979.

136. Neal R. Peirce, "The 'Third Place' in Our Lives: Could it Be a Mall with a Soul?" *Washington Post*, n.d.

137. Hardwick, *Mall Maker.*

CHAPTER 8

138. Rouse-Randhurst Shopping Center Intra-Office Memorandum, April 2, 1982.

139. Letter from James Rouse to Victor Gruen, June 14, 1973, as quoted in Hardwick, *Mall Maker*, 212.

140. "Living: He Digs Downtown," *Time*, August 24, 1981.

141. Ibid.

142. Kathleen Meyer, "Randhurst Center Dolls Up to Recapture Customers," October 16, 1983.

143. Ibid.

144. Ibid.

145. Press Release, "The Picnic Opens at Randhurst Shopping Center," MPHS Collection.

146. Ibid.

147. Press Release, September 25, 1984, MPHS Collection.

148. John Slania, "Mall Keeps Pace with the Unexpected," *Daily Herald*, May 26, 1989.
149. Jean P. Murphy and Mary Hagen Wajer, "Mount Prospect: Where Town and Country Met," 1991.
150. "Mall Keeps Pace with the Unexpected."
151. Ibid.
152. "Mayor Welcomes 15 New Stores to Randhurst Shopping Center," *Chicago Suburban Times*, November 22, 1989.

CHAPTER 9

153. Victor Gruen, *The Heart of Our Cities. The Urban Crisis: Diagnosis and Cure* (New York: Simon and Schuster, 1964), 195–98.
154. John Slania, "Randhurst Mall Still Shines on Silver Anniversary," September 13, 1987.
155. John Mullin, "Randhurst Just Won't Give Up," *Daily Herald*, April 15, 1992.
156. Ibid.
157. David Roeder, "Randhurst Embraces New Store Offerings," *Daily Herald*, June 4, 1995.
158. Erin Holmes, "First on the Mall Block, Randhurst Still Holds Its Own vs. Woodfield," *Daily Herald*, June 28, 2001.
159. Erin Holmes, "Randhurst Unfazed by Closings," *Daily Herald*, December 30, 2000.
160. Pam DeFiglio, "H2Oh!" *Daily Herald*, October 12, 2004.
161. Matt Dormis, "New Look Coming for Randhurst," *Mount Prospect Times*, April 29, 2004.
162. Matt Arado, "Randhurst Plans an Open-Air Era," *Daily Herald*, August 14, 2003.
163. Ibid.
164. Ibid.
165. Steve Zalusky, "Randhurst to Get a Makeover?" *Daily Herald*, April 30, 2007.
166. Ibid.
167. Sue Ter Maat, "Randhurst Revamp Wins Board's Approval," *Daily Herald*, August 20, 2008.
168. "A Fond Farewell for Randhurst," *Mount Prospect Times*, January 1, 2009.
169. Zalusky, "Randhurst to Get a Makeover?"

APPENDIX A

170. "History of Market Square," http://www.historicmarketsquare.com/page2.html.
171. "Park Forest, IL," *Encyclopedia of Chicago*, Chicago History Museum, http://www.encyclopedia.chicagohistory.org/pages/957.html.
172. Tim Cronin, "Former Shopping Landmark to be Demolished," *Southtown Star*, October 26, 2010. Available online at http://www.southtownstar.com/neighborhoodstar/matteson/2835324,102610fields parkforest.article.
173. Village of Park Forest, http://www.villageofparkforest.com/index.php?submenu=Downtown&src=gendocs&ref=DownTownHome&category=Downtown.
174. The Plaza, History Section, http://www.theplazamall.org/plaza.php?page=history.
175. "HIP History: Then and Now," http://www.shopthehip.com/flash/history/html.
176. Westfield Old Orchard, History Section, http://westfield.com/oldorchard/centre-information/history.
177. Gruen, *The Heart of Our Cities*, 198.
178. Labelscar Retail History. http://www.labelscar.com/illinois/golf-mill-shopping-center.
179. DuPage County History, http://www.dupagehistory.org/dupage_roots/OakBrook_16.htm.
180. Oakbrook Shopping Center, http://www.oakbrookcenter.com/about.
181. http://chicagoist.com/2010/10/21/u_of_c_grad_seeks_funding_for_docum.php?gallery0Pic=6.
182. Malletin.com, http://www.malletin.com/malldirectory/Ford-City-Mall/5369.html.
183. Wikipedia, s.v. "Yorktown Center," http://en.wikipedia.org/wiki/Yorktown_Center.
184. Lakehurst History Web Resource, http://www.lakehurstmall.net/history.html. (This is a great website that I highly recommend visiting.)
185. International Council of Shopping Centers, http://www.icsc.org/srch/sct/sct0504/page43.php.
186. Labelscar Retail History, http://www.labelscar.com/illinois/lincoln-mall-matteson.
187. Malletin.com, http://www.malletin.com/malldirectory/Northbrook-Court/5373.html.

188. Deadmalls.com, http://www.deadmalls.com/malls/orland_park_place.html.
189. Jamie Lynn Ferguson, "Orland Park Place Left a Success," *Orland Park Prarie*, October 27, 2008. Available online at http://www.opprairie.com/Articles-c-2008-10-27-186639.112113_Orland_Park_Place_left_a_success.html.
190. Labelscar Retail History, http://www.labelscar.com/illinois/the-malls-of-downtown-chicago.
191. John Revelle, "Lakehurst Forever," http://lakehurst.webs.com/mallhistory.htm.

About the Author

Gregory T. Peerbolte has worked in public history for over five years and currently serves as the executive director of the Mount Prospect Historical Society in suburban Chicago. He holds a degree in history from Illinois State University and professional certificates from Northwestern University and the University of Chicago. His hobbies include music, artwork and the Chicago Cubs and Bears.

www.ingramcontent.com/pod-product-compliance
Lightning Source LLC
Chambersburg PA
CBHW070357100426
42812CB00005B/1538
9781540229663